Copyright © 2014 by Ann Anovitz

Published and distributed by ✠RICHER Press
An Imprint of Richer Life, LLC

4600 E. Washington Street, Suite 300, Phoenix, Arizona 85034
www.richerlifellc.com

Cover Design: Richer Media USA
Photographs: Big Stock Photo and 123RF

No part of this publication may be reproduced, stored in a retrieval system, or transmitted in any form or by any means, electronic, mechanical, photocopying, recording, scanning, or otherwise, except as permitted under Section 107 or 108 of the 1976 United States Copyright Act, without prior written permission of the publisher.

RICHER Press also publishes its books in a variety of electronic formats. Some content that appears in print may not be available in electronic books.

Library of Congress Cataloging-in-Publications Data

Anovitz, Ann

Charlie's Tale
The Great Mystery
Ann Anovitz -- 1st edition
p.   cm.

ISBN 978-009903391-9-0 (pbk : alk. Paper)
1. Spiritual 2. Philosophy 3. Self-Help

2014954617

ISBN 13: 978-0-9903291-9-0
ISBN 10: 09903291-9-0

Text set is Adobe Garamond
First edition, November 2014

Printed in the United States of America

╬RICHER Press
An Imprint of Richer Life, LLC

RICHER Press is a full service, specialty Trade publisher whose sole goal is to *shape thoughts and change lives for the better*. All of the books, eBooks and digital media we publish, distribute and market embrace our commitment to help maximize opportunities for personal growth and professional achievement.

To learn more visit
www.richerlifellc.com.

CONTENTS

Introduction — 7

PART I

Chapter 1 — 11

Chapter 2 — 21

Chapter 3 — 47

PART II

Chapter 4 — 63

Chapter 5 - 1860 — 73

Chapter 6 - Summer 1863 — 91

Chapter 7 - Fall 1863 — 113

Chapter 8 — 129

PART III

Chapter 9 — 139

Chapter 10 — 143

CONTENTS

PART IV

Chapter 11   197

Chapter 12   203

PART V

Chapter 13   215

AFTERWORD   219

ABOUT THE AUTHOR   221

Charlie's Tale

INTRODUCTION

This tale is simply my own thinking about the great questions of life and death. Where am I and why am I here? What purpose do I have on earth? Is God in His own time working to civilize man? What future does He have in store for us? Will we ever learn to love and care for each other … or will we die like the dinosaurs?

My friend Sylvia and I have been studying the Old Testament for over six years and have had deep and prolonged discussions dissecting the thoughts presented.

I hope *Charlie's Tale* gets you thinking, reading and discussing.

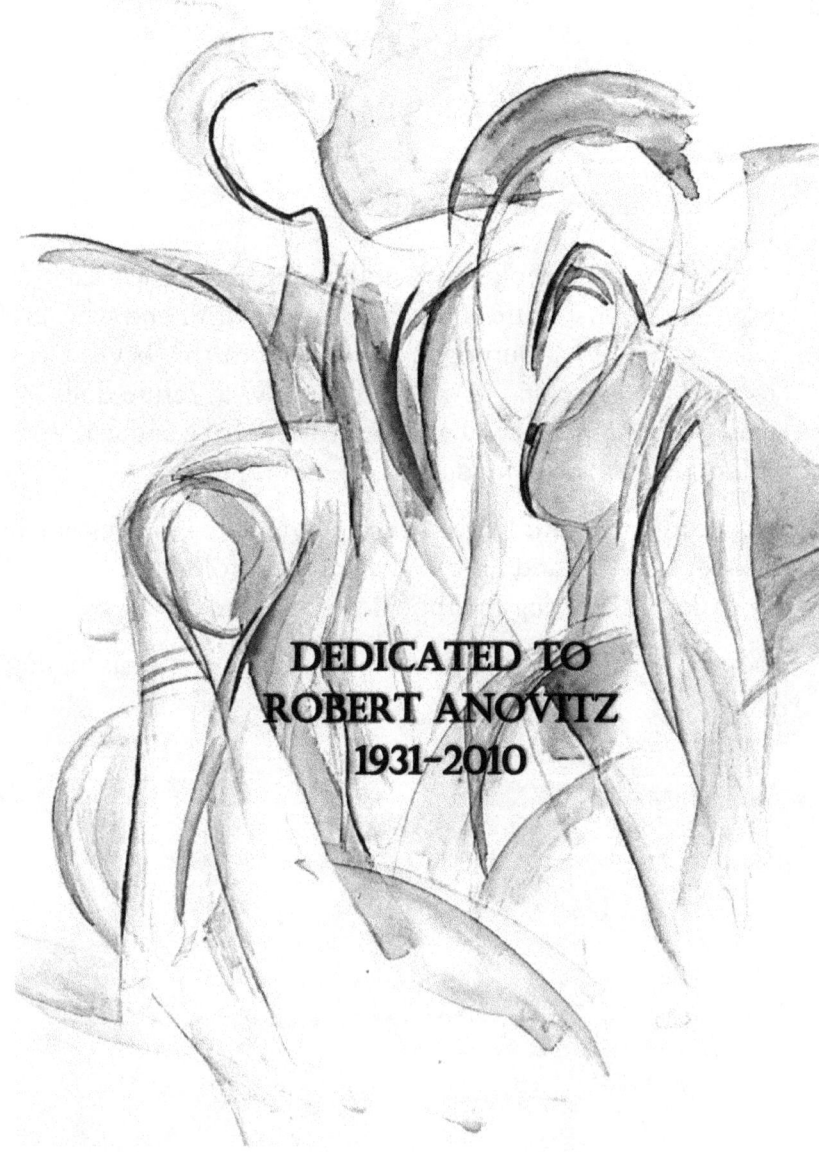

DEDICATED TO
ROBERT ANOVITZ
1931–2010

Charlie's Tale

PART 1

Charlie's Tale

Charlie's Tale

CHAPTER 1

What the hell? *The lights just went out! In the middle of the game? I was just sitting at the park eating my dog and drinking a cold beer. The Yankees were beating the Sox, but, hey, the Sox had two on base and the Big Guy was up. Now, all of a sudden, it's pitch dark. No game at all. Wait a minute, I do see stars. Gee they're pretty. Good grief, here I am in some weird place and thinking about stars. But, hey, I don't think they're all stars. There are some kind of lights or fires out there.*

You know, I think I've seen something like these lights before; sort of quick out of the side of my eyes. I was thinking maybe I ought to see an eye doctor, that maybe it was a cataract. But this is different; almost as if some of the light was coming from me.

Whoa, it is coming from me! Good Lord, I'm on fire! Help, Fire! Fire! Now just a minute, Charlie. You're not really on fire. Just calm down.

Charlie looked around and realized he was looking at a lot of other firelights, all colors; red, green, yellow and everything in between, floating gently in the quiet darkness. *Am I one of them?!*

My body is just light! I'm not seeing with my eyes! So how can I see? What's going on here?!

Charlie's Tale

At that moment, he felt the comforting warmth of a nearby orange light. Within the light he saw a slim, familiar figure.

"Don't I know you?"

"Sure, Charlie. You better know me," came back the answer. Not really a voice, more like a thought.

"Dad? "

"You got it, son!"

Charlie rushed to hug his Dad, but ended up hugging nothing but a warm light. He backed off, looking at his Dad, strangely.

"Dad, what's happened to me? Where are we? What are you doing here? I thought you were dead! But boy, am I glad to see you. Is Mom here too?"

"Well, you could say I am dead, son. You too. But, don't fret. You'll get the hang of it. And yep, your Mom is here. I'm sure you'll see her later on."

"Holy cow, Dad! I'm dead? No, no, that can't be. I'm just 46. I can't be dead! How did I die? What's going to happen to Julie and the kids? How are they going to get along without me? The kids are so young. They're only eight and ten. I gotta get back. Do something Dad. Tell them to send me back!"

"No can do, Charlie. Dead is dead. But Julie and the kids will be okay. They'll pick up your construction contracts and do just fine."

Charlie's Tale

"Oh, God, what am I going to do?"

"That's right, Charlie. You have some work to do. It all has to do with God."

"Oh, don't kid me, Dad. This is bad, real bad."

"It's not a matter of kidding you, Charlie. You have a lot of work to do here to heal your soul, and like I told you, Julie and the kids will be fine. You'll be able to check on them a little later."

"Well maybe. Julie's a strong woman. She helped me with the business when we first got going. But I got a lot of stuff to do. There are a lot of contracts on the burner."

"Like I said, they'll be fine. As for what happened, think back to the park and see if you remember anything."

"I remember"... *Hey buddy, that'll be two dogs and two beers for my friend and me. . . . Thanks, keep the change. This is a great game Joe."*

"Yeah, thanks for the dog and beer, Charlie. How's the family doing?"

"Oh, you know. The kids are running in and out all the time, Julie is busy working for that engineering company, taking care of the house, the kids, the PTA and volunteering at the hospital. I hardly see them, except on Sunday at church."

"And how's business? Did you get that contract for the new electric power building downtown?"

"Yeah. I fudged on the price, cut it by 15%, cause I know I can make it up and get that money back by putting in for extras during the job."

Charlie's Tale

"You're really good at this bidding thing, Charlie. You don't think it's wrong?"

"No, Joe. A man's gotta look out for himself, you know."

"Yeah, Charlie, you are so right."

"How about you, Joe? How's your business these days? "

"Doing okay, Charlie, except Mona's on me all the time to take the kids to lessons and ball practice and she's got me painting the house now."

"I just tell Julie I'll get a round to it when she asks me to do something. And if she asks me to take the kids somewhere, I pretend to be asleep in my chair."

You got it made, buddy."

"Wow! Look at that hit. Go, Go, Go, slide, slide, you bum."

Whoa, Charlie, calm down. Your face is really red. You feeling okay?"

"Got a little heart burn from that last dog, I think. But I'm o...kay...

"You see, son, you had a heart attack, right there in the ball park. They called the paramedics but you were gone by the time they got you to the hospital."

"Good grief! I wasn't feeling so bad, just a little indigestion from the hot dog. Sure, a little too much stomach from a little too much beer, but, dead?"

"No exercise either," his Dad reminded him. "You used to go bowling every week. What happened to that?"

Charlie's Tale

"Yeah, I belonged to a league with my friend Bill Watson. When Bill's army reserve unit was called up, the team let me bowl for the both of us so we could keep his place. But when Bill was killed by one of those road bombs over there, I just couldn't keep going. I would think of him every time I went to the bowling alley. So I dropped out."

"That's too bad Charlie. Bill was a nice guy and a good friend of yours."

After a quiet minute thinking about Bill, Charlie shook himself. "Well, Dad, am I in heaven or someplace else? If I'm in heaven, where's God and the angels?"

"You're kind of nowhere and everywhere, son. Heaven isn't like people think. What we have here is a place for learning, kind of like a college, where your soul will learn what it's missing so you can draw closer to God."

"Just how in the hell am I supposed to do that", Charlie asked angrily. "You know I never was much for a lot of studying, just made it through high school. And what are we? What's with all the different colored lights? They look kinda like fire flies only bigger."

"Right now, Charlie, your soul is at the lowest level of consciousness, just in from earth. You're a pale yellow. As the soul learns and grows, it takes on a different color, like I'm a deep orange. The highest levels are those brilliant blues out there in the universe. Your mom is a bright blue now. She was a very good lady during her life-time."

Charlie's Tale

"Well, okay, so what do we do now?"

"Come on. I'll introduce you to somebody who'll help you through all this."

His dad moved off and somehow Charlie found himself following. *"Will you look at that sky!* It's *a dark, sapphire blue, with all those brilliant stars. And, in between there's millions of firelights, floating around. The moon looks so close; I could reach out and touch it. And the earth! Wow! I can see everything."*

His dad led him toward a bright red light and introduced him.

"Charlie, this is Meg. Meg, this is my son, Charlie. He just arrived."

Within the light, Charlie could see the image of a beautiful, young woman with huge blue eyes and golden curls.

"I've been expecting you, Charlie. Are you comfortable?" she asked kindly.

"That depends on what you mean by comfortable," Charlie grumbled. "I don't hurt anywhere, but this sure is strange. I feel kinda…shaky."

"Yes, this does take some getting used to."
"It sure does. I can't believe it."

"I'll see you later, Charlie," his dad waved as he drifted away.

Charlie cringed. "Don't leave me, Dad. This is scary."

"I have to take care of some things Charlie, but if you want me, just think of me and I'll be there for you."

Charlie's Tale

"Well okay, I guess. It was sure good to see you again. Say hi to Mom if you see her."

Charlie turned back to Meg. "So what happened to you Meg? You're so young. How did you die?"

"I was in a car accident, Charlie. Hit by a drunk driver. I went just like that!"

"Wow, that's terrible. I guess I drove when I had a little too much too. Lucky I never hit anyone."

"Yes, you were very lucky. You see, my husband and little girl were left alone. It still hurts to think about how they might be getting along without me."

"Yeah, I know I'm worried about how Julie and the kids will do without me too."

Charlie gave himself a shake. "So okay, what am I supposed to do now? How do I go about this learnin'?"

"I have all the records of your life right here," Meg answered, waving a bunch of papers at him. "You weren't real bad, Charlie. You worked hard for your family. You loved them very much. You all went to church together every Sunday. And, you took care of your mom and dad before they passed on."

"On the other hand, you cheated people, Charlie, people you had business with, even your friends and family. You were thoughtless and self-involved, didn't pay attention to the needs of other people. No one lives alone, Charlie. It's all about how we deal with and get along with others. You didn't really listen to God's message. In fact, you usually snoozed through the church service."

"But, let's start with some questions. I see your son Jimmy plays baseball. Did you ever coach for him or any of the teams?"

"How could I. I was always too busy working," he said defensively.

"How about your daughter's hockey team?"

"No, but I did get to see both kids play once in a while," he snapped back.

"Uh, huh. And when your neighbor across the street hurt his back and was laid up for months, did you help him out?"

"How do you mean?" Charlie asked, unsure what Meg was getting at.

"Did you mow his lawn, take his dog for a walk, or offer to take him to his doctor appointments?"

"I guess not," he replied scratching his head. "But hey, I had to make a living. I can't be going around spending time for nothing."

"Oh, I know, Charlie. We all had to make a living. I worked for an advertising agency."

"How about when you went hunting and left all that trash? You weren't too particular about taking care of the woods, were you? You know God gave us the whole world with its animals and plants to take care of."

Charlie's Tale

"Well, I wasn't about to put all that trash in my car," Charlie sputtered.

"And what about the contracts you padded and the material you skimped on in your construction jobs, Charlie?"

"Not so good huh? But I had to beat out the other guys if I wanted to get the contracts. What should I have done? If you don't cheat a little, you don't get the business."

"How about your wife, Charlie? She's a nice woman, helps out at school and at the veteran's hospital even though she works all week. After work she comes home, makes dinner and helps the kids with their homework. But, what do you do? Yes, you work hard all day, but then you come home, take a bottle of beer from the refrigerator and sit in your favorite chair watching a TV sports channel till dinner. Then it's back to the chair for more sports or the newspaper until bed time."

"Yeah, so what's wrong with that? I work hard and it's the women's job to take care of the house and the kids."

"Even though she also works hard all day?"

"Well yeah. A man's got to be a man, right."

"You didn't really listen to your wife and kids, when they wanted to tell you about their day or what happened at school. You only pretended to listen. I can see where you need to learn a few things, Charlie."

"You asked your father about God. I guess you thought if you came to heaven you would see God and his angels. But,

Charlie's Tale

it doesn't work that way. There are many things you didn't learn on earth during your life. Many people you hurt or just didn't think to help. You need to change, Charlie. You need to grow up and have a deeper understanding of what is expected of you as a human being. Then you can become one with God. Then you will know Him," Meg said, patting him on the back like his mother used to do.

"Well just how do I go about this learning, Meg?" Charlie asked in exasperation. "Like I told Dad, I was never much for school. Suppose I can't or just don't want to 'learn' anything. What happens then?"

"You don't want know, Charlie. Take my word for it," she grimaced. "But this will be a very different kind of school. Here's what I think we should do. We'll get you started with visits to a couple of planets in other galaxies so you can see how other life forms live. Would you like that?"

"I suppose so, but how will I do that?" I don't even know how I got here? Will it be dangerous?"

"I'll send you on your way and don't worry no one can hurt you now. I think we'll have you visit one place here in our Milky Way and another in a far galaxy. You'll find these places very different from earth and from each other. When you come back, we'll talk about what you've learned. Bye, Charlie. See you soon."

CHAPTER 2

O*h, my God! I'm flying and it's pitch black out here. It feels like my bedroom when I was a kid and Mom turned off the light. It was so dark I couldn't even see the walls. I felt like I was driftin in a universe of blackness and something was out to get me. But here I am, flying through this real, dark universe.*

Wait a minute now, Charlie. It ain't so dark. The sky is filled with bright planets and stars. Hey, some look like ice cubes and some have gas shootin up all around. I remember in astronomy class they said the planets don't sparkle. The sparkling ones are stars like the sun. Gee, Charlie, I guess you did learn something in school.

This is sure different than anything I expected. That Meg is a nice lady, pretty too. Too bad about how she died. You don't think about things like that when you drive after drinking with a bunch of friends. After what we see in the news, we should know better.

Here I thought I was a pretty good guy, but I guess an average Joe ain't good enough for heaven. And anyway, why should I have lived any different? Why should I have to help my neighbor? I'm tired after work. I just want to relax. And I don't remember Julie ever saying nothin. She did hand me a 'honey do' list once in a while, but I musta lost 'em. Somehow though, she got everything done herself. And the kids was always running in and out or bickering with each other. I'd yell at them

Charlie's Tale

Charlie's Tale

to slow down or shut up! I never knew what they were up to. . . . Well, alright, maybe I should have asked.

As for work, heck, business is business. You want to make a buck, you got to do what you got to do. Scam on the bids and cut on the materials. It's the only way to come out ahead.

Besides, who would a thought I'd die so young. I never thought about it. People don't think about dying till they get older. I never even thought about it when Mom and Dad passed on.

And now, here I am, flying along to God knows where and I'm supposed to learn something? I guess we'll see just how much they can knock into this thick head of mine.

It's pretty strange not having a body. I don't feel anything touching me, like all these rocks floatin' around. Though I did feel a kind of warm air coming off of Dad and Meg.

Uh oh, I'm gettin awful close to that planet up ahead. Hey, it looks a lot like earth with all them blue and green and tan colors.

With a final swish and a little breeze, Charlie stepped down lightly onto a lovely meadow, covered in flowers. Huge blankets of yellow, red, orange, purple, white and every color in between. The shining sun was a deep orange. It was evening, the sky was a pale peach and the air smelled delicious.

This don't look so bad. Listen to them bees buzzin' and just look at them butterflies. There must be millions of 'em.

Charlie's Tale

Suddenly several butterflies came right up and landed on a startled Charlie. Then they started talking! "Whoa", he gasped.

"Hello, Spirit. Your colors are rather dull, not very pretty at all, and you're as big as our brothers and sisters but you have no wings," said one little butterfly tickling his ear. "Come on with me and meet the rest of us," it invited, and off it flew.

"Spirit? Well I guess I am. I sure don't have my old body no more. At least my back don't hurt none now, so there's something good about being dead."

Charlie figured he had seen some strange things so far, so what if butterflies could talk. So he followed along and saw they were headed toward a huge forest that made the horizon a bright, green haze against the brilliant, peach sky.

Nearing the edge of the forest, Charlie saw people approaching. *Thank God, some real people. That's a relief.* But, as they neared, he stopped short. "Yikes! You're not people! You're human-sized butterflies! I must be seein' things. Oh my God, look at your colors; you're all like rainbows," he exclaimed, astonished.

"Hello Spirit," one answered in a friendly way. "From where do you come? How can we help you?"

"Oh my God, it talks too. Just look at you. Your wings are all shades of blue with black and yellow and white in between. And you've got the prettiest golden eyes, even got black

Charlie's Tale

antennae growing out above 'em. But at least you have human arms, legs, hands and feet. What are you anyway?"

"Why, we are butterflies, Spirit," the big fella explained.

Charlie swallowed hard and got a hold of himself as he stammered. "Uh, my name's Charlie, Mr. Butterfly. I come from earth; that's the 3rd planet from the sun in our galaxy. At least that's what I heard on that TV show, Third Rock From the Sun. And I'm supposed to learn something about you folks."

"Then you are welcome, Spirit. I am called Blue. I'm not familiar with the names of the planet and galaxy you mentioned, but we are glad to have you with us. God has sent us other creatures from time to time, but you are the first from your planet."

"So you folks believe in God too? Well, back on earth, I died and my soul ended up in the sky somewhere and I thought I was gonna' meet God. At least, what I was taught back on earth was if I was a decent guy and didn't do bad things I would go to heaven. But it sure isn't like I thought it was gonna' be. They gimme' a helper named Meg, who tells me I got a lot to learn to be a better person. I thought I was a pretty decent guy, ya' know. But, I guess I did a lot of things wrong back on earth. Sure, I didn't go out of my way to help other people and I suppose I didn't do much for my folks, but how much can a guy do? Am I gonna' have to work in heaven? This is really confusing."

Charlie's Tale

"Charlie, we believe that every living thing is a part of God. That's why we work together and take care of everything on our planet. We believe nature is the very essence of God."

"That's a real nice way of looking at things, Blue."

"Come with me now, Charlie. The sun is setting quickly. You can nest with us during the dark."

Charlie followed Blue and the other butterfly people into the forest, only to have his mouth drop open as Blue flew up into a large tree and rested in the crook of a branch.

"Uh, hello up there. Where am I supposed to sleep? I don't think I can fly; I don't have wings and I ain't gonna' climb no tree." Charlie called. We humans can't fly back home, except in machines called airplanes."

"Oh, I'm sorry, Charlie," Blue called down. He motioned to a nearby gold and orange butterfly that came over to help lift Charlie up into the tree.

"This is pretty comfortable," Charlie announced, settling down on a branch. "Is this your home?"

"This is where I sleep when it is dark. When it is light again you will tell me what is home." And with that, he closed his eyes, folded his wings around himself and was silent.

Charlie nestled between two branches and tried to think about all the questions he had. But he found his mind closing down and he was soon asleep, knowing nothing more until the first faint light filtered down through the leaves of the trees.

Charlie's Tale

"Good daylight to you Spirit Charlie," Blue said as he helped Charlie down from the tree. "Would you like something to eat?"

"Blue, I don't know if a spirit can eat. But I'd like to try."

"Well, will you look at that! All the butterflies are laughing and talking and digging into that huge, wood bowl filled with seeds and honey." Charlie laughed. He reached out and found he could take some and even put it in his mouth, or at least where his mouth had always been.

Hey, if I can eat, maybe I can fly too. This new self of mine is very interesting, he thought as he enjoyed the taste of the honey rolling around his mouth.

This is good stuff, a little stronger than our honey. But, it ain't like the hot dogs and beer at the ball park. Or the barbecued ribs we had on summer Sundays at home. I'm gonna' miss all that.

"Boy, this honey tastes great Blue," Charlie said, running the sweet treat over his tongue. You must have bees here."

"Oh, you must mean our stings," laughed Blue. "Yes they are our little helpmates."

"My grandpa used to keep bees," Charlie mused. "I remember, as a kid, putting on a funny mesh helmet, and a long-sleeved shirt and gloves and going out with him to get honey from the hives. The bees would buzz all around, but didn't attack. I guess they were used to grandpa. After we cleaned off the hives, we'd go into the kitchen and spread

Charlie's Tale

honey all over grandma's pancakes. Wow, that was good! I miss those times. I miss home."

"Tell me, Charlie, what is this 'home' and what is your planet like? Are all the life entities like you?"

Good grief. Where do I even begin? How am I supposed to tell this guy about everything on earth? Oh well, here goes nothing. . . .

"Okay, Blue, to begin with, we humans don't sleep in no trees. We got houses, four walls and a roof. We call that home." For a second, Charlie found himself thinking longingly about his home, Julie and the kids. Shaking his head, he continued. "And, we stay in our homes with our wives and children except when we go out to work or play."

"What is work and play?"

"Uh, hm, work is what we do to make money. Uh, money is a kind of a trading material we use to buy food and a home and other things we want. Play is what we do when we're not working. We might play ball or ride a bike or play cards when we're resting from work but not yet sleeping. We sleep in the dark time too."

"This is all very interesting, Charlie. Explain ball and bike and other play."

Oh, boy. Charlie looked around. He picked up a bunch of leaves and flowers, crushed them into a ball and threw it, remembering how he and his Dad used to toss the ball around on hot summer days.

Charlie's Tale

"That's one kind of ball," he said, sadly, remembering that he hadn't played much ball with his own kids. "One person throws the ball and another hits it or catches it. As for a bike, well let's see." He looked around again and picked two round daisies.

"See how these flowers have petals all around to make a circle. We call that a wheel. Some people make wheels where they work. Then we put a seat on top of the wheels and ride around. That's a bike. It's a lot of fun."

Boy, I wanted a bike when I was a kid. But we never had much money for extra things. Oh, dad made a living, but things were always tight. So, I got odd jobs helping the neighbors mow their lawns or bagging at the grocery store until I saved up enough for a bike. What a beauty she was, red with white stripes on the fenders, hand brakes too.

"We make all kinds of things that use wheels Blue, like cars that take people from place to place, but they move a lot faster than bikes."

"Cars?" questioned Blue.

This ain't gonna be easy Charlie, he thought, impatiently. *This place is really something different.*

"Uh, I'll tell you about cars later, Blue."

"All right. Charlie, do you have other life forms like our Stings?"

"Oh, sure, we got Stings too, but we call them bees or wasps. And we got four legged cats and dogs that live with us. And there are a lot of four legged animals that live in the wild away from us humans. We got birds and butterflies and fish that live in the ocean. Do you have oceans and rivers, big areas of water?"

"Oh, yes. We call them wets. We have both large and small wets. I have much to show you, Charlie. Take my hand and we'll fly together."

Charlie took Blue's hand and they rose gently into the air, gliding over miles and miles of flowers and trees. The morning sky was now a pale pink. They flew over bright green lakes and rivers and forests of dark green trees that stretched from horizon to horizon.

The air felt warm and smelled great and he felt so free, not afraid at all.

"This is the most beautiful thing I've ever seen. I bet our planet used to look like this. God sure knows how to make things right, doesn't he."

"Say, Blue, while I think of it, we have places back home, buildings we go to every Sunday to worship. Our pastor, talks about good and evil and how we should follow God's Commandments so we'll go to heaven when we die. But I'm usually taking a snooze during his sermons. Do you have a place everyone goes to worship?"

"Not a specific place, Charlie. We believe that our whole planet and everything on it is one entire place of worship."

Charlie's Tale

"Ah, here we are. Let's stop by this wet, Blue suggested. You can meet the swimmers."

They landed neatly on the bank of a large river. Charlie figured it was algae like the stuff in the park pond back home that made the river look so green. Blue called out in a soft, singing sound and pretty soon a human-like fish walked right up out of the water. Charlie stared goggle-eyed. It had a human body with fins along each arm, webbed hands and fins attached to the back of webbed feet and along the length of its back. There were also gills behind its ears and it was all wrapped in a rainbow of iridescent color that flashed in the bright sun.

"Fin, this is Spirit Charlie," introduced Blue. "He is a new soul visiting around the universe."

"Welcome, Charlie," Fin exclaimed. "Are you enjoying your visit?"

"Oh, I'm havin a great time," Charlie shook his head, grinning. "It's so beautiful here and no buildings or trash to mess things up."

"Would you like to join us underneath for a while?" Fin asked.

"You mean under the water, uh, wet?" he asked suspiciously.

"Sure, you're just a soul, not a living creature."

"Yeah, well I guess so then. What about you, Blue?"

"I'll wait for you here, Charlie. I can't breathe in the wet."

Charlie's Tale

Charlie eased into and under the cool water with Fin. As his senses became accustomed to the dimness he saw hundreds of fish people like Fin. But there were other creatures as well. Some, with hard shells, swam or crawled on the river bottom eating sea flowers and algae. *They look like our crabs and lobsters*, he thought. There were some fish that looked very much like the ones back home and what seemed to be family groups gliding about.

"Hey, Fin, those fish are all talking and laughing with one another like we do back home."

"This is really something. Since it looks like you can be in the water and on land, how much time do you guys spend in the water and how much time on land?" Charlie asked.

"We spend about three quarters of our time in the wet. But my school often goes on land to forage for different foods or to visit with the other creatures."

"Oh, my God, there's a shark! Look at those teeth, will ya'. We better get out of here."

Fin laughed. "Don't worry, Charlie. That's just my pet, Lagoona." Fin whistled and the shark swam right up to them.

"He won't hurt you, Spirit. Come pet him."

Charlie looked sideways at Fin as he eased reluctantly up to the great fish and touched its nose. But the shark gave a flip of its tail and swam off into the depths.

"Now that was neat," he laughed.

Charlie's Tale

"Lagoona likes his tummy rubbed," Fin chuckled.

"Hey, look at all the minnows over by that rock. They're so still. What are they doing?"

"They are young trout learning how to forage," Fin answered.

As they swam through the cool, dim water, Charlie realized he was feeling very peaceful in this different dimension. There was plenty of light from the sun at this depth. The colorful, exotic creatures and rock and coral formations were absolutely beautiful. It was amazing. *I could easily stay down here forever and be happy*, he thought, lazily.

Slowly Fin guided Charlie deeper. There was almost no light in the murky depths. But just as Charlie began to feel concerned and a little queasy, a group of neon fish swam by.

"Gees, Fin, those fish are glowing. How do they do that?"
"They have special light cells in their bodies, Charlie. The Lord God thinks of everything."

As he swam along, Charlie reflected on what Fin had just said, recalling the special features many creatures had back on earth; the antlers of the deer and elk, the odor of a skunk, spots or stripes for camouflage. *HE gave us humans our five senses and a brain. I guess like Fin said, God thinks of everything.*

Charlie was about to relax on a smooth rock, when some kind of huge fish came gliding by.

"Oh, God, Fin, that fish just ate a whole family."

Charlie's Tale

"Yes, Charlie, we all have to eat. He had to eat them to survive. Surely your life forms have to eat."

"Of course we do. But we humans mostly grow our own food and raise animals to eat. But, now I'm thinking about it, I guess the wild animals have to hunt just like that fish. You know, Fin, we also have some bad people who kill wild animals just for the fun of it. Sometimes people even kill other people for no reason at all or because they want something another person has," Charlie admitted.

"I don't think we have such creatures here, Charlie."

Charlie and Fin relaxed for a while, just floating in the water. Charlie enjoying the sensation and the quiet watched the coming and going of the underwater scene. *This is much better than watching TV and much more relaxing*, he thought. Then Fin called over to him. "Ah, Charlie, I hear Blue calling. I'll take you back up now. I'm so glad you came to visit. Join us any time."

"Thanks Fin. That was super. I learned a whole different view of life."

They rose slowly up out of the river to find Blue who was perched on a shady tree limb

"That was so neat, Blue. Thanks for bringing me."

"I gave him the full tour, Blue. He especially got a kick out of my pet shark, Lagoona, Fin laughed, disappearing under the waves."

Charlie's Tale

Charlie joined Blue who was now sitting under the tree and thought about the lives of the fish he had seen.

"You know, Blue, at home I like to go fishing. We usually eat what we catch. 'Course they're not made like Fin; more like those small fish in the river. The real little ones we throw back so they'll grow bigger. After this though, if I ever get a chance to fish again, I think Ill have to throw all of 'em back. I never thought about fish being like people, having families, laughing and talking to one another."

As Blue sat glistening in the sun, Charlie started thinking again about all the creatures he had seen. *I never really thought about animals having feelings and a brain that could think about their place in the world. As far as I was concerned they were either just pretty to look at or something to eat.*

"Say, what are your people doing today, Blue?"

"They are gathering food, Charlie. We collect seeds and help the Stings collect sweetness from the flowers and then we all share. That's how we sustain ourselves."

"I guess gathering food would be your work then. What else do you do during daylight?"

"We clean our nests, bring water from the wets, tend the plants to make sure they are comfortable and have room to grow, and take care of the children. Would you like to see the children, Charlie?"

Charlie's Tale

"Sure, Blue." They flew over to a group of trees with large leaves and pink flowers. As they neared, Charlie saw a group of butterfly people hovering around.

"What are they doing? Where are the kids?"

"They are watching the children," answered Blue. "At this stage the children are very hungry and their job is to eat as much as they can before their next stage. They're right in front of you, Charlie."

"Stage? Well, I'll be," he laughed. "This tree is crawling with caterpillars; all kinds of caterpillars. Of course! The children are caterpillars before they turn into butterflies, just like on earth."

"Yes and we are watching them so the flights don't eat too many."

"So, these flights, they're your enemies?" Charlie asked. "Do you have to fight them off and maybe kill them so they won't eat your children?"

"Oh, no, the flights are not something to fight. They mostly eat the seeds from the flowers and trees and take only the weak children, those who fall from the trees, and the elderly who can no longer collect," Blue explained.

"And you don't call them enemies, eating the old people and children who can't help themselves?" Charlie asked, astounded. "Well, if they're not your enemies, who are?"

"I don't think we have any enemies, Charlie, at least if you mean something that will purposely hurt or kill us. We all live

Charlie's Tale

together and help one another. If the flights didn't eat the weak there would be too many of us to share the food."

"That's pretty hard, Blue. We try to share with people who don't have enough food. Shouldn't taking care of everything on the planet include caring for people? How can you just throw these kids and the old folks away? Don't you have doctors and hospitals to take care of them? Don't you care?"

"Yes Charlie, we care. It's sad, but necessary. But, what are doctors and hospitals?"

"Oh Lord, you don't even know. . . ."

Just then Charlie heard a piercing scream. "Oh, my God! What was that?! What was that scream, Blue?"

Things started happening rapidly. The butterfly people turned their faces to the trees and spread their wings around the children, trying to protect them. The bees and insects gathered in swarms. Blue took Charlie's hand and pulled him up into a tree with what seemed to be an instinctual reaction rather than panic or fear.

"What the heck's going on, Blue?" an alarmed Charlie asked.

"A bad one is attacking, Charlie. Keep your head down until it goes away."

He heard more screeching and looking down saw a large orange butterfly dive-bombing at the butterfly people who had either settled on the ground or in the trees with their wings covering them. The bad one as Blue called it, kept strafing them and trying to break through swarms of bees and butterflies to get to the food.

"What in the world? Tell me about this 'bad one', Blue. What is it doing to you folks?" Charlie asked worriedly.

"We have beautiful trees and flowers of all kinds here, Charlie, but there is one tree we don't go near," Blue informed him. "The flowers are poisonous. Even the smell can make us become a bad one. Some of our people become too curious, smell the flowers or eat of the fruit. Then they become bad. They will not gather or share. They take from everyone else and sometimes one of us gets hurt or even killed. They try to get our food.

"If one is bad, we turn our backs, do not let them share and they eventually die. In the mean time though, they can make a lot of trouble."

"That's pretty extreme. But, I guess no worse than what happens on earth. We put bad ones in jail; a special building where they have to stay or if they are especially bad we kill them."

"Your way sounds pretty extreme too, Charlie."

While they were talking, the screeching and pounding went on. The noise was deafening. Charlie saw one of the butterfly people fall from its place on the tree and disappear into the tall grass. The bees and some of the larger butterflies attacked the bad one and finally drove it off and there was quiet again.

Charlie's Tale

"What happened to the butterfly that fell, Blue?" Charlie wanted to know.

"The bad one probably ate it," Blue stated matter-of-factly.

Charlie shivered, if you could call it that in his present condition.

"I get it, Blue. Like this is the tree of knowledge thing we got in the Bible. One rotten apple can destroy everything. I'd sure call him an enemy."

Gradually things went back to normal. No one seemed too upset; even losing one of their kind to the bad one didn't seem to upset anyone.

As they came down from the tree Charlie asked about that. "I don't understand, Blue. Don't the rest of you feel bad about your friend who was eaten? Don't you want to help the bad one? Our doctors are especially trained people who work in hospitals buildings where they try to fix hurt ones or bad ones."

"No, Charlie. This is our life and we accept these things as necessary."

"Well I never would. I'd be darned upset at being attacked. I think I'd go after him to protect my family. Or maybe first I would try to help him so he could be cured.

At least I could take him to a doctor." *Yeah, Charlie, like you helped your neighbor?* he thought sarcastically.

Charlie's Tale

As they walked through the meadow, Charlie saw that everyone was back at work.

"So, Blue, you got work time and times when you're attacked, but don't you guys ever play? What do you do in your free time?"

"Free time? We don't have free time, Charlie. We are always busy."

"How about new things? Who thinks up new ways to make work easier or who thinks up ways to heal the sick? And, I know you got wings and don't need mechanical things to get around. But you must want stuff."

"No, there's nothing we want, Charlie. We are happy just the way things are."

Well, I guess if you're happy the way things are and don't have many enemies, what do you need to make new things for, thought Charlie. *But then, everything stayin' the same all the time wouldn't make for a very interesting life. On the other hand, they got enough to eat and nobody much to be afraid of. They keep the place real nice and help each other. What's not to like? Still, I think I'd be bored to death. No bowling, no ballgames, no TV. And I don't like the idea of just letting the sick and weak die without at least trying to help. In that way I like our planet a lot better. Though I guess I didn't do much about helping others, like my sick neighbor or Julie and the kids.*

"Oh, Charlie," Blue interrupted his thoughts, "here come the flights I was telling you about."

Charlie's Tale

Charlie looked up and saw a large flock of red balloons with small flipper-like wings and long blue and yellow feathery tails heading toward the meadow.

"Look at that, I thought they were balloons, but they're really birds with long necks and small heads," Charlie observed excitedly. Huge eyes seem to take up most of their heads except for those long, thin, golden beaks.

"Their beaks remind me of our humming birds' only so much longer. Our humming birds are very tiny, Blue, only about an inch long."

Charlie and Blue sat down in the middle of a field of flowers and watched the flights as they slowly dropped down, ate some flowers and seeds and then seemed to rise back up into the air.

"How do they do that, Blue?" They don't exactly fly; they just rise up and down like balloons."

"It's the air, Charlie. When they come down, they rise again with the warmer air and the winds blow them around the planet."

"Gees, I never saw anything like the creatures on this planet. Hey, are they singing?" Charlie had expected these giant birds to be really loud, something like crows. Instead he heard a soft, trilling.

"Yes, that's their call," Blue explained.

Charlie leaned back on his elbows watching the flights and the smaller butterflies drifting among the flowers. *This is wonderful,*

Charlie's Tale

he thought. *The larger butterfly people soared up around the flights and down again to the flowers. How very beautiful, like a giant dance on a huge stage. I really didn't appreciate the beauty of our world. Whenever I was outside I was always going somewhere. If I was hunting, playing golf or even if I was mowing the lawn, I never stopped to look and enjoy.*

I do remember some things from when I was a kid, like when it snowed and we ran outside to make tracks through the yard or build a snowman or a fort. The air was so crisp and clean, the snow so white it sparkled. And when I woke up in the summer, the birds were singing and the air coming in through the window was so fresh. Then I'd eat mom's great breakfast and run out to play baseball with my friends. That was pure joy but, of course, I didn't appreciate it then.

Just look at these flowers, will you. Julie would love them. She always wanted me to help her put flower beds around the house. Why didn't I? I didn't have time? No, I could have made time. One less beer after dinner, read the paper later. She was right. The house would have looked nice with roses next to the front porch. I could have. I should have. It would have made Julie happy, he thought sadly.

Blue took Charlie's hand again. "We had better get under the trees, Charlie. The wet drops will soon be coming. They come for a short while every day."

"I love this flying, Blue. Your wet drops are what we call rain, every day, huh? Do you have snow or ice when it gets cold?"

"Explain snow or ice."

Charlie's Tale

"I guess you don't have any, or you'd know. It's when it gets very cold and the rain drops turn hard, icy, pile up and cover everything with white stuff."

"It does not get cold here," said Blue. "Though it does get warmer and then we fly to the other side of our planet for a time. That gives the plants here time to refresh too." Charlie thought the climate seemed idyllic, but remembered how much he loved the changing seasons at home.

The two of them flew under a large tree and watched the rain come down. By Charlie's estimate, it lasted about an hour.

"I'm gonna have to think some more about you folks and your planet, Blue, cause it seems to me if everything here is the essence of God, you would take better care of the old folks and the weak ones, try to help them and maybe even try to help the bad ones. Come to think of it, I haven't seen any old folks around. I guess they've all been eaten by the bad ones.

"You know, Blue, maybe we have to not only obey God's Commandments but actually 'do something' to help others, not just our own people, but everything on earth including the animals and plants. After all, like you said, we were put on earth to take care of everything on our planet?"

"You may be right, Charlie. Maybe my people should spend some time thinking this through. Maybe we are meant to learn something from you, too."

Charlie's Tale

The rain stopped, the sun came out, and Charlie felt himself being gently pulled away.

"Gee, Blue, I think they want me to move on. I'm gonna hate to leave you folks. This is such a pretty place, but I guess I gotta go learn some more."

"I have enjoyed meeting you, Charlie. You've given me a lot to think about. I'm sorry to see you go. I hope we will meet again sometime. Please take these seeds with you as our gift and plant them somewhere in your travels."

Charlie took the seeds, waved at Blue and the other butterfly people and was suddenly whooshed out into space.

Well, that wasn't so bad. In fact, it was pretty darn nice.

So, here I am again, flying around the universe like it was nothin at all, he chuckled as he whooshed in and out among the debris.

And, the creatures I just met. They live their lives, co-operating with one another. They keep their planet clean and nice. They're very happy living as they do. On the other hand, they have no interest in anything new or any reason to want things to change. They care only about creatures like themselves. The old, the weak, the ill are left to fend for themselves. No inventions, no medicine, no new foods. No play, no competition.

Remember Charlie, no wars either.

He compared their lives with his own. Were their minds different or was it just a matter of where and how they lived?

Charlie's Tale

I was like that back home, Charlie thought. *Didn't think about other people, never went out of my way to help anyone, not even my own family. Why? I never thought about it? Too lazy? Maybe just too stupid.*

Then Charlie was jerked up like a hand had taken hold of the back of his shirt, and hurled far out into the darkest part of the sky. Pulled deeper and deeper into the void, he passed through millions of pieces of rock, huge boulders and even larger masses the size of planets.

Oh, God! This don't look so good, he thought. *What's in store for me now?* He was frightened thinking about what might be in store for him in this, cold, dark part of the universe.

Charlie's Tale

CHAPTER 3

Charlie felt himself falling fast toward one particular, dark, giant planet. He slammed down hard.

SPLAT! Holy cow, some landing! Good thing I don't have a real body anymore, I'd be mush.

Despite feeling a constant pull toward the ground, Charlie finally managed to stand up. *Pretty strong gravity. This planet seems to be made of some dark, hard, shiny material; not much color anywhere; just a few gray patches here and there.*

The sky was inky dark, though he could still see stars. No moon, no sun. *Wow, it looks cold here,* Charlie thought, trying to rub his arms. That didn't do much good. He'd forgotten he had no real body.

Jagged mountains with deep canyons rose around him. Huge boulders were scattered everywhere, pushed by what looked like lava flows. Several of the mountains were obviously still active volcanoes, spouting steam and rock.

What was that?! Charlie thought he saw something moving. Turning slowly toward a particularly large rock, he watched a truly strange apparition emerge. It crept slowly toward him pulsing different colored lights. As it drew near, he saw the creature was round, almost flat, with black and tan spotted fur

Charlie's Tale

covering all of its body except its head. It was the head that was flashing.

The creature had arms and fingers similar to humans, but its legs and feet were more like a tortoise, short and splayed out. It stopped about ten feet away, pulsing rapidly. *What the heck! He's talking with those light flashes!*

"OK, bud. What are you doin in my territory? Nobody comes here 'less I say so."

Charlie was stupefied. "Hey, I'm just passing through. I'm not going to hurt you."

"As if you could," the creature flashed.

"I came to see your planet and find out what lives here. Don't worry, I won't be staying long; mind if I tag along and ask some questions."

"Yeah, I mind. But since the souls up in heaven sent you, I guess I'll have to put up with it. What do you wanna know?"

"I'm Charlie. What do they call you?"

"Muffin."

Muffin? Charlie managed to stop a snicker. This didn't look like any muffin he ever saw. "Uh, Muffin, are there any more of your kind here? What about other life forms? What do you eat? Where do you live?"

"Whoa. Not so fast. Come on, let's move while we talk. It ain't safe here."

Charlie's Tale

"Waddaya mean it's not safe; why not?"

"The Grays or the Stripes might attack and I gotta patrol my territory. But, before we talk about me, tell me about the place where you lived. I've heard from other visitors that everything stands straight up tall trying to reach your star. Is that right?"

The heavy gravity made for slow going, so as they made their way around boulders and down steep sided craters, Charlie told Muffin something about earth and how he had lived and how the force of gravity was very different.

"You see, Muffin, our planet holds us close too. We call it gravity. But, it doesn't pull nearly as hard as yours does. Then too, our star is very bright and hot. Everything that grows on earth needs the sun light to make its food and grow. I guess that's why things on our planet reach up toward the sun.

"I have a mate called Julie and two kids, uh, offspring we have created. We call the boy Joe and the girl Jean and we live together in a nice house. While our children go to school every day to learn about our world, Julie and I go to work to earn a living. Julie works for a company that designs bridges to go over water and I build buildings for people to live and work in.

"I guess Julie is trying to take care of my business now. I sure hope she's doing well and customers are paying her on time.

Charlie's Tale

"But, now, it's your turn. Who are these Grays and Stripes and why would they attack you."

"Cause they want my territory, that's why. And I want a certain sweet little spot the Stripes have. So, I'm gonna go after it. I got my bombs all ready and my neighbor, Juice is gonna help. We're gonna fight the good fight. This piece of land is right between us. 'Course then I'll have to take it from Juice, but that can wait a while. First though, I gotta make sure my slaves have put up enough weapons for the fight."

"Slaves, why do you have slaves? Who are they?"

"They're some spooks who came over here from the next planet. Have a hard time livin' here, but good enough to do some work. I'm gonna check on 'em now, so you'll see for yourself."

They started climbing up the slope of a high ridge. As they moved around another large boulder, Charlie saw the bright light and sensed the heat coming from the crater of a large volcano. Red hot lava was bubbling up and running slowly down the mountainside.

The shadows of some sort of creatures played out against the glowing lava. They seemed twice as tall as he was, but were bent almost double by the pull of the planet's gravity. An icy white, they had no hair anywhere on their bodies that he could see, heavy lidded eyes with just slits to see through and hands and feet like flexible paddles.

Charlie's Tale

"Well look at that! Some of your slaves are tending plants and some kind of wriggling worms along the cooler areas at the edge of the crater. Others seem to be taking some of the molten rock and pouring it into molds. And those guys over there are pulling buckets of water up from the river below to pour around the worms and plants."

"See, this is what I need 'em for," said Muffin.

"Don't you have more of your kind to work with you, Muffin?"

"No, I don't trust 'em. They got their own places and slaves."

As they watched, one of the slaves slipped and fell into the red hot lava. He made no sound as he burned. But Charlie felt an agonizing shriek in his head. The other slaves gathered together nearby, holding their heads as they watched their friend burn to death. Charlie could feel their horror in his soul.

"My God, Muffin, does that happen often? He burned to death!"

"It don't happen often. I've only lost three of 'em. But now their gonna waste time, stop work and have a ceremony. I tell you, Charlie, I can't get much work out of 'em, stopping all the time for ceremonies," Muffin said, shaking his head in disgust.

"But, everything looks about ready. Hey, you. Yeah you, Jones, stop with the ceremony already. Fill the wheelbarrow with bombs and spears and come with us. Come on, Charlie, we got a ways to go. The Grays and Stripes live up on the high places and we gotta get close."

Muffin and Charlie, with Jones following behind with his wheelbarrow, moved slowly toward some distant peaks.

"I see you got some rain and snow here, at least at higher elevations. Looks like snow up on those hills," Charlie noted.

"Yeah, rains pretty often. I try to stay out of the snow. It gets too deep for me," Muffin answered.

It took them a while but they finally climbed about half way up the side of one of the mountains where Muffin stopped, breathing heavily.

"Charlie, you're too bright. They'll be able to see us coming. Go hide behind those rocks over there. Jones, you stick with me and bring the wheelbarrow."

Charlie crept behind some large boulders and watched Muffin pick up one of the bombs. He couldn't believe what he was seeing. Muffin's arm stretched out like a rubber band as he hurled the rock about five hundred feet. *Wow, wouldn't it be neat if I could throw like that. I'd be the greatest pitcher that ever played the game,*" he thought.

Muffin threw a second rock and then Charlie saw the Stripes. Large round animals that looked like giant porcupines were crawling along the ground. "Well I'll be! They got long, sharp, black and white quills covering their bodies. I guess that's why they're called Stripes.

Charlie's Tale

Their eyes were hidden behind the quills and they had tiny arms and legs with many fingers and toes attached to each. As Muffin went for another rock, they started shooting quills at him and Jones.

The Stripes were shouting and hissing. Quills, rocks and spears were flying everywhere. Charlie found himself ducking even though nothing could hurt him. When he next peeked over the rocks, Muffin was firing rocks with one hand and spears with the other. Jones had crept under the wheelbarrow and was rolled up into a ball. Something screamed; someone was hit. Muffin looked like he was being overwhelmed.

Charlie jumped out from behind his rock, grabbed a spear and threw it as hard as he could. Another scream! He'd actually hit someone! Then he realized what he was doing? *Just like everybody back home. We get carried away and join in even when we know it's not right.* He crept back into hiding, disgusted with himself.

With everything flying back and forth, Charlie wondered how long the fight could last. Muffin was running out of weapons, and there were fewer and fewer quills coming at him. Then suddenly it was quiet. Muffin was growling. Jones crawled out from under the wheelbarrow.

"Who won?" Charlie shouted over to Muffin."

"That louse Juice never showed. I'm gonna wring his neck. Nobody won. Now I gotta do this all over again," answered an angry Muffin. "But I gotta get some rest first and make some more bombs. Then we'll try again."

Charlie's Tale

'We,' thought Charlie. *Not if I can help it!*

"Say, Muffin, do you have a house?"

"Nah, but I got a nice little cave with some good drips. Come on, we'll get some sleep. You hungry? Want some worms?"

"No," said Charlie, thinking about eating worms. "I don't need food anymore."

Before they had gone very far though, Muffin hollered, "Get down." Arrows were flying over their heads. They lay flat on the ground. Then Muffin pushed Charlie down over the edge of a small crater and followed him in. "It's the Grays," he moaned.

Charlie looked up and spotted some large, flat, gray beasts with small heads sticking up from very long necks. These heads consisted mostly of large, bright blue eyes that bulged out and swiveled like antennae.

"They can't see very well, advised Muffin. None of us can because it's so dark here. We use our sense of smell. And they have those big antennae eyes that can find us anywhere."

Charlie watched the Grays use some kind of big bow they held out straight in front of them while they pulled back on the rope with their teeth. "Why aren't you shooting back?" Charlie asked.

"It don't do no good. They got some kinda thin shield covering them and everything bounces right off. Only their heads ain't protected. We just gotta stay here till they run out of arrows. They won't come any closer cause we can kill em if we hit their heads."

While they waited, Charlie thought about how far these creatures had developed. *Boy, these guys have invented the ways and means to fight. They have slaves to take care of their food and water needs. Why, in a couple, five hundred years they'd probably have nuclear bombs.*

After a while, the Grays disappeared and Muffin and Charlie were able to walk back to the volcano where they settled down in a large cave about halfway up the hill. Jones walked off, pushing the wheelbarrow toward the other slaves.

"Muffin, your slave, Jones, he never said a word."

"They don't talk to us. But, I think they might talk somehow to each other."

Charlie nodded. He couldn't watch Muffin eating his worms, so he kept his eyes on the flowing lava outside the entrance to the cave.

"Muffin, did you folks always live like this, fighting each other? At least, didn't you Spots ever live and work together?"

Muffin munched along and thought for a while before answering. "The old stories tell of a time before the great explosion when we were part of a larger planet. There was light then they say. We had clans with like creatures living together and we worked and traded with the other species. But there was always suspicion and some fighting going on.

Charlie's Tale

Then came the big explosion and we found ourselves blown far out in the universe, away from our star."

"You said you folks know about heaven and God? I don't think God would approve of you keeping slaves or so much fighting, Muffin."

"Oh yes, we know there's a God. We just don't think he's very interested in us, so why should we listen to him. They say long ago He gave us some rules to live by. But where was He when we needed him, when our star exploded, and where is He now? You didn't see Him help me win the fight just now, did you? No way."

"We have wars too, Muffin, but I don't think God likes fighting. And, did you ever think of letting your slaves go?"

"Go? Where would they go? They can't take care of themselves. I give 'em food and someplace to stay, so they work for me. They would die if I let 'em go."

"Are you sure of that?"

"Sure I'm sure. I'd go after 'em and kill 'em if they left. I need 'em. Ya see?"

"Yeah, I see," Charlie answered

After a minute, he asked, "But, Muffin, do you worship God in some way? Like, we get together in a building called a church every Sunday to pray and talk about good and evil."
"Yeah, we got us the Great Stone at the meeting place. Every year we sacrifice to the God of that stone so it will protect us from any more planet explosions."

Charlie's Tale

"What do you sacrifice?"

"One of the slaves, of course. One clan antes up one slave each year. See we take turns. How's that for cooperation? Wouldn't do to sacrifice one of ourselves, now, would it?"

Then another question occurred to Charlie. "Muffin, with all this fighting, how do you mate? Don't you have children?"

"Oh, we mate alright and have kids too. We have a truce while we're all together at the sacrifice. We eat and drink, and dance up a sweat with the priests and after the sacrifice we meet up with someone to mate. The females take care of the kids till they can eat on their own. Then they kick 'em out and send them over to us. We men teach them to fend for themselves and how to fight. And we make sure nobody hurts them while they're little kids."

After he finished eating, Muffin curled up for a nap and Charlie sat quietly musing about the planet he was on, how different it was from Blue's but how alike it was in some ways to earth, like the slaves and the fighting.

I wonder if the hardships of this planet have encouraged the selfishness, suspicion and fighting and if all of that has led to change and innovation? These folks had to invent ways to protect themselves and fight off invaders. They had to think of ways to get food and water because they couldn't grow anything here.

After a while, Charlie began wondering how the slaves felt about things. "Well, okay, Charlie, get up and go find out", he told himself.

Charlie's Tale

Charlie left the cave and climbed up the side of the volcano, looking for Jones. Finding him sitting on a large rock, Charlie sat down beside him.

"Hi, Jones. How's it going?" he offered. "I'm real sorry about your friend dying. But maybe he'll become a Spirit like me. That's not so bad."

Jones picked up his head and looked questioningly at Charlie but said nothing.

"Can you guys speak – communicate, uh sign even?"

Charlie felt more than heard an answer. The message came directly into his mind but felt like singing rather than spoken words.

"Oh yes, Spirit. We can communicate. Thank you for thinking of our friend. What would you like to know of us?"

"Oh, my, Jones. That kind of tickles," Charlie smiled. "Tell me, how did you get here? Isn't there some way for you to get back? And why don't you speak to Muffin?"

"Muffin simply does not want to hear. As for our planet, it is cold and dying. Worse than this planet since we are further from our sun. We have little food and nothing with which to build shelters and keep warm. My friends and I were set out to look for a suitable location where we would find welcome for those of us who are left. Our method of transportation is not mechanical but is a matter of two minds connecting to move one physical entity."

Charlie's Tale

"Unfortunately, since we arrived here, we have had no communication with the others on our planet. We do not know if they still live or if something here disturbs the communication. We are waiting. In the meantime we live and work."

"What about how Muffin treats you and how the others treat their slaves? Doesn't it bother you? Aren't you angry?"

"No Spirit. How we live is of no matter. Muffin thinks of us as slaves, but we do not feel that we are slaves. If and when we wish to leave, we can and will. In the meantime, work is good and we eat and keep warm. When the Lord of all things wishes something to change, it will."

"So you believe in God, then."

"Yes, we know HE IS."

"I wish I could help you, Jones, but I'm only a Spirit. I wish you and your people well. Now, I guess I better get back to Muffin before he wakes up and wonders where I am."

Charlie ambled back down the side of the volcano thinking about Jones and his people and what God had in mind. *Why doesn't God help all his creatures. Why doesn't He put out His hand to fix things that are bad?*

In the old days the Bible says he spoke directly to the people. Does he speak to us now, but we don't hear? Does He have a larger reason for not helping us whenever we need him? I guess there's no way we can ever know, he decided.

Charlie's Tale

As he approached the cave and the just waking Muffin, Charlie felt himself being called back to heaven again. "Well, Muffin looks like my time's up here. I'm being called away."

"Ya know, Charlie, it was kinda nice having you here, someone to talk to and show around. I'm sorry to see you go. I hope I taught ya something."

"Oh, you did, and, oh Muffin, try to be nice to your slaves. They do understand and communicate. They might even be able to help you," he said as he waved good-by and was whisked away from the dark planet.

Well, Charlie thought, *all that fighting doesn't seem to do these creatures much good. Yes, they think, invent, change their environment to some extent. But, they are only solitary people who take no comfort or pleasure with each other. How very sad.*

It's really kind of sad that I didn't make more friends when I was alive. I used to have friends at school and we had a ball together. Why didn't I keep up with them? Why didn't I make more new friends? Was I afraid someone would want something from us?

Charlie's Tale

PART 2

Charlie's Tale

Charlie's Tale

CHAPTER 4

Charlie just coasted along this time and after a while came upon the familiar red light that was Meg.

"Hi, Meg," he called.

"Charlie, glad you're back. I'm about to leave."

""Leave? Where you goin'?"

"There's been a big explosion out near the Cigar Galaxy and many souls have been called to help. We're going to have an extra large group to orient to their new surroundings."

"You mean there are regular people, like more humans, out there in the universe?"

"Well, maybe not what you would think of as regular, Charlie, but souls are souls, whatever they look like."

"Yeah, I guess so. But say, how often does this happen?" he asked bewildered.

"Not very often, usually when there's war, famine or plague.

Then things get really hectic. But this time there was an earthquake and a mountain erupted. People weren't prepared and many died," she said sadly.

Charlie's Tale

"Does everybody go? What about me? Do I just wait here till you get back?"

"Oh, no, not all of us go. We're just called as needed. But, I have a great replacement for you. You're going to be very happy. Here she comes. See that beautiful blue light?"

"Mom! Mom am I glad to see you! You look so young and beautiful. It's been such a long time.

"I wish I could hug you, but that didn't work so well with Dad." His mom laughed. *She looks so young and lovely, he thought. Her hair is dark brown, not grey any more.*

Charlie's mom was a short, plump little lady with a self-confident, warm smile. *That's the smile I remember.*

"See you later, Charlie," called Meg as she flew off. "Bye, Meg," Charlie called after her. "Thanks for calling on my mom to help me and thanks for being so patient," he called as he turned back to his mom.

"Mom do you know about my life after you died; Julie and me getting married and the two kids?"

"Yes, Charlie, I know all about your lovely family. I often drop in on the children. They're so beautiful. Of course, they don't see me, but I think they can feel me around them. I'm really sorry you died so young, Charlie. You grew up to be a pretty good man but you still have a lot to learn. I know you're worried about your family, but Julie and the kids will be fine."

Charlie's Tale

"So Dad told me. That's good, but I wish I could be with them one more time."

"Maybe someday, Charlie."

"Boy, seeing you brings back memories, goodies in my school lunch box, your great cherry pie. And you were always there with a cool hand and chicken soup when I was sick. You used to read me stories and even poetry before I went to sleep. And remember how we used to look in the closet and under the bed to make sure no monsters were hiding before you closed the light?"

"I love you Mom. Oh, and Julie could never match your cherry pie," he chuckled.

"I love you too, Charlie," she smiled. "Now, I understand you've been out and about the universe. Why don't you tell me about it?"

"What a trip. First I went to a beautiful planet with butterfly people and talking fish. Can you believe that? They had a wonderful life cooperating with one another. They shared everything and believed their entire planet and everything on it was a part of God. But, ya know, Mom, since everything was so great, they didn't really have to think.

Or maybe their minds just didn't work that way. They didn't have any use for anything new not even new ways to do old things; no need to invent anything. They didn't need or want anything else; just accepted life the way it came. They even accepted their weak and old folks dying – not even trying to

Charlie's Tale

help them. I couldn't understand that, especially since they were such nice people."

"Oh, Charlie, don't you realize you were the same way about people. When I was sick and you stopped by, you hardly stayed a minute. You couldn't leave soon enough."

"I guess that's right, Ma. I couldn't stand to sit there and watch you. I never could stand staying around people who were sick or hurt but it wasn't because I didn't care about you."

"I always wished you could have been with us more, Charlie after you left home."

"I'm sorry, Ma. I wish I could change a lot of things I did or didn't do back then," he said sadly. I can see now how empty Blue's planet felt without love. And, they never got the thrill of inventing something everyone could use or the good feeling you get taking care of people who need you. They had nothing to challenge them, not even playing games for a little fun. For the most part everything was pretty dull."

"I'm glad you can see that, Charlie. Your life was pretty dull too. Working, coming home to eat, watching TV and going to bed. You didn't get the thrill of seeing your kids play at their games or enjoy the companionship of your wife and friends very often."

Charlie nodded sadly. "I see what you're saying, Mom."

Recovering himself, Charlie went on to tell his mother about the second planet he had visited.

Charlie's Tale

"The other planet I went to, Mom was really something different. It was very dark, cold and far out in the universe. The creatures there didn't cooperate at all, barely even with their own kind. Each one lived alone except for his slaves. Yeah, they kept slaves, Mom, creatures from another planet who had found their way there.

"Where did the slaves come from, Charlie? What were they like?"

"These folks were really interesting, speaking kinda mind to mind. They had landed on that planet looking for a new home since their own planet had lost its sun. They believed that God was guiding them and they'd eventually find a new, welcoming place to live. Meantime, Muffin, one of the strange creatures who lived on this particular planet treated them terribly, forcing them to work and do what he wanted.

"Don't you see, Charlie," his mom interrupted, think about how you treated the people who worked for you. You paid them as little as possible, gave them only one half hour for lunch and no other breaks during their days of heavy construction labor. You did not think about them or their families at all. In a way, you even treated Julie like a slave, expecting her to do everything with the house and kids with no help from you."

"I guess you're right, Mom. I never thought of it that way. I know I should have helped Julie. I was just too lazy. And the guys at work, "I guess I should of given them a couple of breaks during the day and maybe longer vacations," Charlie

Charlie's Tale

said as he ran a hand through his hair and rubbed his face thoughtfully.

"Anyhow, talk about differences with Blue's planet, Muffin and the other people on their planet were always fighting with each other over territory, food and water. They didn't trust anyone, not even their own kind. They didn't share anything."

"Kind of like a lot of people on earth, don't you think, Charlie?"

"Yeah, I guess so. We are still making war on each other. We've tried though, Mom. I hope the people on earth learn to live together. But you know, I think maybe it has to start with neighbors getting along with neighbors, Mom, accepting the differences. You know, live and let live."

"Now you're talking, Charlie. Good for you!"

"Hey you know, I didn't even want to ask Muffin how his people mated. But he told me they met once a year to sacrifice to some stone god and that's when they mated."

"The females took care of the kids till they could find food for themselves and then the men taught the kids to fight and looked out for them until they were ready to go off on their own."

"These guys believe there is one great God, Mom, but they believe He don't care about them because he let their nice planet explode, so they don't care". What do you think of that?"

Charlie's Tale

"Sad, Charlie, really sad."

"There were other strange creatures on the planet too, but they were always fighting each other and everybody else."

"And what do you make of all that?" asked his mother.

"Ma, I'm really confused. I never thought I was so bad, just like everyone else on earth. But it's easy to see the difference between the two planets I visited. I found myself comparing our world with theirs. I could see how earth is really like both planets and I could see myself in some of the creatures. I wouldn't really like to live on either planet. These creatures don't have no feelings for their own. They just accept everything the way it is without trying to change it for the better.

"It made me think about some of the things I did and didn't do in my life. I wish I had a chance to talk to my kids and Julie. Maybe I could help them better now; at least I would be more involved in their lives.

"Charlie, you are really beginning to see how things were back home. I'm glad for you."

"There are so many choices we have to make in life, Mom. It's hard to know what's right"

"At least you're beginning to think now, Charlie. But you still have a lot to learn to begin to understand the meaning of God."

Considering a moment, Charlie said, "You know Mom, in some ways that cold, difficult planet was way ahead of the beautiful planet that was so easy to live on. Maybe if there is no hardship there is no progress. But there is fear and hatred and constant fighting on Muffin's planet. While the people on the beautiful planet are so comfortable there is no progress at all."

"You're right about that, Charlie. Now, part of what you have to learn is about other people in other countries on earth, how they relate to God, why there is so much evil in the world, why people can't get along with each other and the part organized religions play. "

"I guess so. What about the different ways people worship Mom? Which religion is right? The two planets I traveled to have rules to live by, but they certainly didn't have all the answers. We have rules to live by too, but most of us barely think of stuff like that. Most of us don't even take church seriously, maybe because we know even the church people are just people who make the same mistakes as everybody else. "

"You have learned quite a bit though, Charlie. Have you noticed your color has changed to a nice bright orange?"
"I never noticed. That's good, right? I am beginning to learn some things. At least I have a lot of questions, but I still don't think I was so bad compared to some of the people I knew back home."

"That may be true Charlie. But right now it's you we have to worry about. At least you have a chance to change. That's why you are here. So keep an open mind."

"Okay, Mom, so where am I going next?"

Charlie's Tale

"Next you're going back to earth. You'll be living as a human in different times and places and you'll be a part of the communities you're living in. Your job will be to learn about the differences between societies and people on earth, how they relate to God, why there is so much evil in the world, why people can't get along with each other and the part organized religion plays."

"And, Charlie, no miracles or anything like that. But you might be able to influence some of the people around you. So think carefully before you try to change anything."

"That sounds like a big job. I know things are different all around our world, but I never studied about other religions and our pastor never said much about those other religions either. How do I go about learning how other people worship on earth? Where am I going? Can I visit Julie and the kids?"

"No, you can't visit as yourself. But you can look in on them and maybe have a chance to influence them, if you're careful. Now, let's do some planning."

"First, you'll go back in time to the Civil War. You will be staying with a farm family called Stillwell, and I think you'll find them and the time they live in very interesting."

"Then, you'll come back here and have a talk with Meg before you go on to your next assignment. I don't know where that will be, but it's certain to be special."

"I love you, Charlie. Now, off you go."

"Bye, Mom. I love you"

Charlie's Tale

CHAPTER 5

1860

The Stillwell family lived on a farm in Western Maryland that had been in the family for several generations. They grew tobacco, hay for the livestock and a kitchen garden for their own vegetables. A few horses, cows, pigs, chickens and a mule made up the stock.

Mother, father and three sons, up at five in the morning, taking care of the animals, a big breakfast at six and dinner at noon. Supper was a light meal and bed not long after.

Mr. Stillwell was a tall, lean man with arms and legs made strong and sinewy by hard work. His face was a study of fine lines, baked in by the sun. He and his oldest son, twenty year old Matt, had black hair and Matt resembled his father though he was somewhat taller. Jess, the second boy, was eighteen, shorter with wider shoulders and lighter coloring. His hair was sun bleached almost white. Johnnie, the youngest at fifteen, was turning out to resemble his father and Matt, but he had light brown hair. And they all squinted alike out of the same steely grey eyes.

The men wore work pants and long sleeved shirts with the sleeves rolled up to their elbows. Floppy, straw or felt hats

Charlie's Tale

with large brims were the order of the day but still, the hot sun bit into them.

When they all came together for noon dinner, the family had some time to talk about what was going on at the farm, the rest of the family spread around the Maryland countryside and anything else of importance. These days there was a lot of talk about politics. At the feed store, Matt had picked up copies of the Lincoln Douglas debates. Douglas was a well-known orator, but talk was Lincoln could hold his own.

The older boys, Matt and Jess were of different minds. "If Lincoln gets elected, there's going to be war," Matt said decidedly. "South Carolina is threatening to secede. Seems to me they got a right to keep their slaves; need 'em to work those cotton fields. Where else they goin to get help? The government shouldn't be buttin' into the States' business anyway."

Jess waived his fork around and spoke over a mouth full of beans. "The Feds got every right. They're not talkin' about slaves. Only some crazies talkin' about slaves. The Feds are talkin' about states rights versus federal government rights. This is supposed to be a union we got us here."

"Well seems to me the Feds ain't got no right to tell the states what they ought or ought not to do. You watch. There'll be war yet."

"Probably so, if South Carolina secedes."

Charlie's Tale

"Maryland's a border state," Mr. Stillwell joined in. "I know lots of people think the south is right, but I don't think Maryland will join 'em."

"You boys hush now and eat up, there's work to be done," put in Mrs. Stillwell.

Ma Stillwell was a small woman with a quick step and a quiet way about her. Her blond hair was beginning to turn grey now and she wore it drawn severely back and tied into a bun at the nape of her neck. Her rough, red hands belied her gentle nature; she was a farm woman, up early, to bed early and never stopping in between. One grey everyday dress always covered by an apron and one black Sunday–go–to–meeting dress with a black straw hat did for her wardrobe.

At Ma's insistence, the talk subsided. Young Johnnie hadn't said anything at the dinner table. He had just listened and thought all those soldiers marching in pretty uniforms with guns over their shoulders was a mighty fine thing.

* * *

Time passed and Lincoln was elected. South Carolina seceded and several other states were on the verge of joining them. They formed a new government called The Confederate States of America with Jeff Davis as President.

Maryland stayed with the union but there was a lot of disagreement among the people. Many agreed the South was within its rights as far as states rights versus the federal government were concerned. Others didn't want a fight between the states. They wanted to keep the union intact.

Charlie's Tale

And then there were the abolitionists in the northern states who were pushing to have the slaves freed.

But, war came. One afternoon, two months after the first shots were fired, found the Stillwells busy with chores. Johnnie was helping Jess shoe the horses. Matt had gone to town for some supplies, Mrs. Stillwell was washing clothes in a big tub next to the well and Mr. Stillwell was out in the fields. Jess's hound, Buford, lay near the barn, snoozing in the shade, then got up, stretched himself and started howling.

Johnnie picked up his head. "There's a wagon coming mighty fast down the rode, Jess."

"Yep. Heard it. Must be Matt."

"If it's Matt, why's he coming so fast?"

"Don't know. Guess we'll see when he gets here."

In a few minutes the wagon pulled to a quick stop next to the barn and Matt jumped off.

"What are you lathering up that horse for?" admonished Jess. An excited Matt caught his breath. "Johnnie, go get Pa. There's a war on." Johnnie turned and ran into the fields.

"Whadda you mean," asked Jess, taking the reins, unhitching the horse and walking him around to cool off.

"Just what I said. Wait till Pa gets here and I'll tell you all about it."

Mr. Stillwell came hustling out of the tobacco with Johnny. "What's going on?"

Charlie's Tale

"We got us a war, Pa. South Carolina has gone and attacked Fort Sumter and the Yankees have called up 75,000 men."

"Let's go inside and talk this through, boys. You best come too, Ma."

Gathered around the table they listened to Matt. "This was all the news they was talking about at the feed store. Last December, the Feds sent in troops to Ft. Sumter out in Charleston Harbor. They figured it's a federal fort so they could do as they pleased. But South Carolina says its sovereign property of the State and the Feds don't have any right to be there. "

"The Seeceshers put up some big guns on the shore and this April, commenced to fire on the fort. The fight lasted about thirty-four hours, they say, and then the Feds surrendered. Now South Carolina is going to secede and Virginia, North Carolina, Tennessee and Arkansas look like they're goin' too."

"Everybody up north is real mad at South Carolina and Lincoln has asked the northern states for more troops to keep the South from seceding. Now, Jess, nobody's talkin about slavery, 'septin those abolitionists, just whether the states have a right to secede."

"Well it ain't got nothin to do with us," exclaimed Ma. "We just got to mind our own business and get back to the chores." She got up and went back to her washing. Matt started bring in the supplies from the wagon and Jess and Johnnie started shoeing the next horse. Pa sat thinking for a

Charlie's Tale

while and then went back to the fields. But later that night after supper, the boys continued their talk.

"They say there was a big 'who ha' in Baltimore when a bunch of troops came through on their way to Washington," Matt told them.

"Like what" asked Johnnie?

"People rioting, the Union army pushing them back, but not liking it one little bit having to fight their own folks."

"Not likely to be any fighting around here, mused Jess. We're pretty far west. Most like to be south and east of here."
"Well I'm going," Matt said decisively. "General Jackson is fixing to put together an army for the South. Soon's harvest is done, I'm leavin'."

"You're goin for the South?" said a surprised Jess. "Why?"

"Seems like I agree with this states' rights thing. Don't see where the Feds have rights above the states."

* * *

Both the north and south called for more volunteers. Meetings were held in Maryland. The Union blockaded Charleston harbor and set up posts all along the Mississippi. There was fighting in Missouri and Virginia. In July, Arkansas, North Carolina, Tennessee and Virginia joined the Confederacy.

And true to his word, Matt left in the fall of 1861, after the harvest was in. Jess went quietly about his work, but Mr. Stillwell was worried.

Charlie's Tale

One day in the spring of 1862, he asked, "What's up, Jess? You're awful quiet these days."

"Been thinking, Pa. I don't rightly see how it would be good for the country if states could secede whenever they didn't agree with the government. Looks like I'm going to have to go with the Union. Can you and Johnnie handle things here for a while without Matt and me?"

"Guess we'll have to if you mean to join up. Where you going to go?"

"Think I'll go up to Washington and catch up with General McClellan's army. I'll leave right after church tomorrow."

"Hate to see you go off to fight, Jess, but I guess there's no stopping you. Have you thought about the possibility you might end up fighting against your brother?"

"That's all I've been thinking about. All I can do is look out for him if we get into a fight with the Rebs. If you hear from Matt, tell him to watch out for me on the other side."

* * *

So Jess left the next day and Johnnie and his Ma and Pa were left to take care of things at the farm. There was plenty to do and they were all pretty tired by the end of day.

Then one Sunday the Reverend Howard asked them to stay a few minutes after church. He wanted to talk with them about something.

Charlie's Tale

"Stillwell, I have a young orphan boy been staying here with me. What with all my traveling around the county, I've got to find him a better place to stay. With your boys away I thought you might could use some help out to your farm. He's a right nice boy, helps around here the best he can, about the same age as your Johnnie. Comes from a farm family over to Hagerstown."

"We could use more help, Reverend. What do you think, Ma? Can we handle another boy?"

"I'm used to doing for four big men; I guess we can handle another boy. You say he's a good worker, not shy to lift his hand is he?"

"No, he pulls his weight alright. This is just no place for him with me gone so much of the time. Name's Charlie Richardson."

"All right, Reverend, let's meet him," nodded Mr. Stillwell. "With the South not producing much and not being able to ship what they do have because of the blockade, there's going to be a real need for as much food as we can grow. This country is going to need every farmer planting every acre he has."

Charlie was now back on earth in the form of a boy of fifteen, in a time and place that was totally unfamiliar to him. *This new body feels great, he thought. No more back pain, knees in good shape again, lots of new muscle. I'm going to hate to give this up.*

Charlie's Tale

He and Johnnie rode in the back of the wagon on the way to the farm and talked about how the fields were planted in corn and tobacco and about Johnnie's brothers joining two different armies.

Charlie told them about a family farm near Hagerstown that was supposedly where he was from. His folks had died of the influenza and he had no other kin. This was all true except for the fact that Charlie was not their son.

The days passed in ordinary farm work and Charlie became like a son to the Stillwells. The boys went to school during the day but found time before and after school to help plant some winter wheat and do their chores.

Mr. Stillwell was very pleased with Charlie and told Johnnie as much. Johnnie said, "You know, Pa, Charlie is real good with the animals. I swear he talks to them and they answer. One morning he told me he thought that old mule, Mr. Bailey, had a bad foot and sure enough when we took a look, that mule had rubbed a sore under his shoe."

"I know what you mean," his father answered. "You watch him and you'll learn a lot about those animals. Why, I saw some butterflies come right up to him and they just lit on his arms like they was talking to him. Never saw anything like it," he said, shaking his head.

Of course, Charlie did speak with the animals. As soon as he saw Charlie, Doc, the oldest of the horses, welcomed him with, "Hello Spirit. It's nice to have you here." The mule shook its head and said, "If you think you're going to make

Charlie's Tale

me work, you got another thing coming. My feet hurt and I'm not about to move." The butterflies were another thing. They came with messages from Blue and Charlie sent back tales of the Stillwells and their farm.

Mrs. Stillwell spent the late summer and fall of 1862 putting up vegetables and fruit while Mr. Stillwell butchered one of the hogs and salted it down for the winter. The boys stored everything in the storm cellar.

"Fighting's getting a might close," Mr. Stillwell noted one evening. "Never thought the Rebs would get this far north. Still think the real fighting won't get as far west as this, but there's bound to be scouts and runaways. Good thing the Reverend stopped by to let us know what's going on. He said Burnside and the Army of the Potomac was fighting Lee over to Fredericksburg and we should be watchful for raiders." "What can we do Pa?" Johnnie asked. "There's no hiding the animals."

"We could spread them out around the farm," suggested Charlie. "Maybe then they won't find all of them."

"Charlie's right, said Mrs. Stillwell. The pigs'll do all right left to themselves; the horses too. Just keep the mule in the barn. Can't do much about the chickens; they're sure to run off with them."

"Yep. That's the thing to do. And it's a might early, but we best bring in the wheat and put as much as we can up in the barn. Get all the stores put in the storm cellar boys and cover

Charlie's Tale

it over with the tobacco covers and dung over that; might keep something that way."

One day, as Charlie plowed he was thinking about this life he was now living. He walked along dreaming behind old Doc turning up clods of good, dark earth. *This is a pretty good life,* he mused. *Working up a sweat over some sweet land, raising your own food and a little more for somebody else. Too bad people can't be happy with what they got.*

* * *

In September of 1862, while the Stillwell family busied themselves with all the extra work on the farm, they heard from a passer-by that there had been a big fight going on in Sharpsburg, just a day's ride east. Lee had made a stand west of Antietam Creek and McClellan had brought the Army of the Potomac up against him.

The fight on September 15 turned out to be one of the bloodiest of the Civil War. The Yankees had 12,000 men killed or missing and the Rebs lost 14,000. A Pennsylvania soldier was heard to say, 'No tongues can tell, no mind conceive, no pen portray the horrible sights I witnessed.'

With both sides exhausted, Lee withdrew and McClellan didn't follow after him. The men of both armies scattered around the countryside looking for food and rest. Nearby farms were pillaged and some were burned. The men of the Stillwell family kept close to the house, keeping a shotgun on anyone going by on the road.

Charlie's Tale

As the armies moved on, things quieted down for the winter. Charlie and Johnnie went out to bring the animals back to the corrals and pens. They found the horses in a forest at the north end of the farm near the mountains.

"Bout time you came, Doc nudged Charlie. We about gave up on you, almost decided to go find us some new friends."

"Thanks for waiting boys. You did a great job hiding. Do you have any idea where the pigs might be?"

"Oh, sure. Saw them down in the gully just yesterday."

"Come on, Johnnie. The pigs are down in the gully up ahead," called Charlie.

"Now, how do you know that? I seen you. Looked like you was talking to them horses. How do you do that?"

"I guess I was, Johnnie. Animals can talk in their own way and I have a feel for what they're saying."

Just then, they saw the pigs and headed them all home. "You're really something," said Johnnie, shaking his head.

The family had tools and fencing to mend and the animals to care for, so they had long, busy days.

Of a winter evening they sat by the fire, Mrs. Stillwell knitting socks and mufflers for the family, listening to the men talk about the war and thinking about her two older sons away in the fighting. Buford, Jess's young blood hound stayed curled up at her feet.

Charlie's Tale

On Sundays the family went to church when the weather allowed and Mr. Stillwell read aloud from the Bible in the afternoon. Charlie listened but seldom said anything. He was listening to the words in a whole different light now.

One afternoon as Mr. Stillwell finished a section, Charlie commented: "You all are Baptists and pretty good church goers. And Ma Stillwell, I hear you sometimes like you're talking away to God, not exactly praying, more like you're just having a conversation. What do you all think about God? Does he answer prayers? Why does he allow war and what the Bible calls pestilence? I been trying to think about a lot of things lately with my folk's dyin' and all the soldiers getting killed."

"Why Charlie, I think that's the most you said since you got here," noted a surprised Mrs. Stillwell, stopping her knitting for a minute. "I suppose I do chat with the Lord now and then. Don't even stop to think on it. Just ask Him to watch over Matt and Jess and the rest of us, and thank Him for what we got. I don't question Him. The Lord knows what's best and we live too short a time on this earth to see His grand design."

"My folks were Methodist and we went to church every Sunday too. Seems to me there's not much difference, maybe more with the Catholics or the Jews."

"Many more religions than that," stated Mr. Stillwell. "There's the Muslims and the Hindus and the Buddhists. Reverend Howard had a sermon once that talked about all the different ways people worshipped. Lot of the basics are the same, like the Ten Commandments, just told a little different."

"The Baptists believe in praising the Lord, don't we?" asked Johnnie.

"I guess they all praise the Lord in their own way, Johnnie. The Reverend and the people in our church like to raise up a mighty shout. I'm told others are a lot quieter about it" answered Mr. Stillwell.

"But there's been so many wars between the different religions, Mr. Stillwell. "Why do they fight each other? Our pastor told us about the Romans and the Syrians pushing the Jews out of the holy land and setting them to roaming around the world, the Crusades and the German Pope fighting with the Italian Pope, and the English King who split off from the Catholic Church because he wanted a divorce so he could marry someone else. What was that all about?"

"Well now Charlie, as far as Christians go, I guess people just think a little different so they go to a church where people believe like they do. The Baptists are a moderate or conservative denomination. We believe in one God, the virgin birth, the sinless life, the resurrection of Christ and the Trinity. We believe in the need for salvation through Jesus.

Most Baptists believe in the 'Four Freedoms':

1. Freedom of the soul to make decisions in the matter of faith

Charlie's Tale

2. Freedom of the local church from outside interference
3. Freedom of the individual to interpret the bible for himself
4. Religious freedom for the individual to choose and practice their religion or no religion and the separation of church and state."

"As for the Jews, our Pastor tells us they believe in the Old Testament. In the old days, Syria conquered Israel, burnt the temple and brought the Israelites to Babylon. But, after about seventy years in exile, a group came back to Jerusalem and rebuilt the great temple. Later, about the time of Jesus, the Romans sent them into exile again. Since the Romans, the Jews have wandered the world, always hoping to go back to their land. They never believed Jesus was the Messiah. But they're still God's chosen people, and the prophet, Nehemiah, believed when the Jews were finally in every corner of the world, that would be the signal for the second coming."

"What did He choose them for?" asked Johnnie.

"Don't rightly know, son. But I think it was to spread the word about one God instead of all the gods like the pagans worshiped."

Charlie was dying to tell them that the Jewish people finally had their home land back after the terrible holocaust of World War II. But, they all sat quietly for a while thinking their own thoughts as they stared into the dwindling fire and then it was time for bed.

Charlie's Tale

* * *

January, 1863 they got word from Reverend Howard that President Lincoln had issued an Emancipation Proclamation, freeing the slaves. This set the family to wondering what effect that would have on the nation, particularly on the South, and what would happen to the newly freed slaves.

"Where they gonna live and how they gonna eat, Pa?" asked Johnnie.

"Don't know, son. Then too, what will the southern farmers do about sowing and harvesting their crops? There's going to be all kinds of "H..." to pay down there.

With spring finally come to the countryside, the family got busy planting tobacco, corn and wheat and Mrs. Stillwell's vegetable garden. Mr. Stillwell also had them plant the fallow acres in beans and beets. He realized there would be starvation afoot in the country.

Once a week, either Johnnie or Charlie road into town to sell Mrs. Stillwell's eggs and produce and pick up the posted news at the feed store. It seemed the fighting had moved on South. Jeff Davis was trying to pull things together despite a lack of men and materials. In March Mosby raided the North's garrison at Fairfax County Court house in Virginia where they took supplies and hundreds of prisoners.

By May, 1863, General Sherman was riding through Georgia aiming for Atlanta and burning everything as he went. In June General Mead with the Army of the Potomac attacked

Charlie's Tale

Lee at Cold Harbor. Lee won a great victory, but it was to be Lee's last major triumph.

One evening in July, at supper, Ma Stillwell said as how she was very worried about her two boys out there in the fighting. "Pa, we haven't heard from the boys in a long time."

"I know, Ma, and I been mullin' over how we're going to bring in the harvest this year. I think we got to go find Matt and Jess. See if they can get away for a while to help us out. Think you boys could find 'em?"

"Last we heard, Pa, Jess was with General Stoughton's group and Matt was somewhere in the Shenandoah with Jubal Early. I guess if we have some luck we could find them. Sides, old Charlie here might be able to get some news from the animals and butterflies. Ain't that right, Charlie?" he chided.

"Oh, I don't know about that, but I'd be right pleased to go help find them, sir."

"I'll sure feel better knowing how they are, Pa, but you think it's safe to send these boys:"

"I reckon if they stay away from the fighting, Ma. You fellas go for the army posts. They should be able to tell you how to find Matt and Jess."

Charlie's Tale

CHAPTER 6

Summer 1863

A few days later, Charlie and Johnnie packed their saddle bags with food and some of the socks and mufflers Mrs. Stillwell had made and tied the bags onto Doc and Lolly. Their blanket rolls went on behind the saddle bags. Mounted, they waved good-by and started down the road. Buford followed after them and wouldn't be sent back no matter how they shouted at him, so they finally just let him tag along.

The boys decided to search for Jess first, and headed to Washington where he had enlisted. They were shocked by all the damage, especially around Sharpsville and Fredericksburg. As they rode slowly through the towns, they passed cemeteries with freshly dug graves and new tombstones glinting icily in the sun. Johnnie's blood ran cold at the sight.

"Jess isn't here," Buford told Charlie who then told Johnnie, and they followed Buford on up the road.

Nearing Washington, they saw soldiers camped around the city and once they got to the middle of town, tents and soldiers covering the entire capitol mall. It was early summer now and the stream that ran through the middle of the mall was nothing more than a stinking quagmire, breeding mosquitoes and overrun with garbage.

Charlie's Tale

But, the trees were in bloom in the parks and along the Potomac River. They were awed by the beautiful white buildings and gawked at the half done capitol dome. Riding by a grand white house, they stopped and asked a soldier limping past whose house it was.

"Why that there's the White House where President Lincoln lives. Works right there too and if you got time to spare, you might even see the President walking over to the War Department next door."

This was nothing new for Charlie, of course. He had been to Washington, D.C. on a school trip and had seen many of the buildings on TV and in the movies. Still, he found it really interesting to get a glimpse of the city at this early date. But Johnnie was overcome by the great city and all the people.

"Where ever do we start looking, Charlie?"

"Let's go to the War Department first," Charlie suggested. "It's that building next to the White House. The other building is the Treasury."

"How do you know that?"

"Well, I just do. Come on."

They tied the horses outside by a watering trough, and Charlie told Buford to keep an eye out for thieves. Lots of civilians and soldiers were going up and down the stairs and in and out of the building and any stray pack animals were commandeered by the army.

Charlie's Tale

"Well, Charlie, since you seem to know everything, where do we go now?"

"Don't know. Guess we'll just have to ask somebody." With that, he walked right up to a couple of officers talking in the lobby. "Excuse me. Can you tell me who to see about finding out where our brother might be stationed?"

"Try the Adjutant's office upstairs, son. They should be able to give you some idea where he's at."

"Thank you," Charlie nodded and tipped his hat.

They made their way up a beautiful marble staircase to the second floor. The Adjutant's Office was teaming with men bustling about and looking very important. It was crowded with all sorts of people clamoring for information. A sergeant acting as clerk was working steadily, but it took most of the day before he got around to Johnnie and Charlie.

"What can I do for you boys?"

"We're lookin' to find our brother Jess, Johnnie replied. Last we heard he joined up with McClellan here in Washington back in '62."

"What's his full name?"

"Jess Whitecomb Stillwell."

The sergeant pulled over one of the large volumes on the counter and commenced to turn the pages, running his finger down the list of names. "Here we go. He was assigned to General Stoughton's garrison over to the Fairfax, Virginia

Charlie's Tale

Court House. But, Mosby raided this past March. Sorry kid, we lost that skirmish and I can't tell you was he killed or taken prisoner. You best get on down to Fairfax and ask around. You might find a buddy who knows what happened to him. I hope he's not in one of the cemeteries."

By then it was late in the day so they parked themselves under some trees in the park across from the White House, ate a little food and bedded down right there for the night along with all kinds of other people temporarily in town. After a while it quieted down. They could see the stars and things felt a little more familiar. The cooking fires had burned down and a couple of men were singing softly.

* * *

At sunrise the next morning they went over to the soldiers' mess on the mall, where they begged some breakfast and some extra bread and jerky to put in their saddle bags. Once across the Potomac and into Virginia, they saw more signs of the war. Closed and boarded up houses and shops, little groups of black people walking north with their possessions on their backs and groups of cavalry riding back and forth on the roads.

"Charlie, where do you think all them black folks are going? They got no place to live now."

"I reckon they think they'll get some help up north, Johnnie."

Charlie's Tale

"You know, Charlie, pretty soon, we're goin to be running into some Rebs. Maybe we should keep off the road and get in the bushes when we hear somebody coming."

"You're right, Johnnie. Least wise till we see whose side they're on. Can't trust anybody if they're hungry or want horses. Keep your rifle easy."

Charlie didn't like the idea of shooting someone. This was a whole lot different then going hunting. But they didn't see anything worrisome and that night bedded down in an old, empty barn just outside of Fairfax, with the horses and Buford nearby.

The next morning they found the Fairfax County Court House. It looked like it had been in a brutal fight. Bullet pock marks all over the walls and doors, windows broken out and the town's people busy trying to rebuild and clean up the mess from the fighting.

They rode up to a large gentleman who was giving orders to everyone and asked if he knew where the Union soldiers were and where the cemetery was laid out. As it happened, they had asked the right person. It seemed that Mr. Churchill was the mayor. He pointed them toward the cemetery.

"You know someone in this fight?" he asked.

"Our brother, Jess, Jess Stillwell. You happen to know him?"

"Can't say's I do. If he's not in the cemetery though, then the Rebs have taken him with the rest of the Yankees down to the prison at Salisbury, North Carolina. You'll find it south and

Charlie's Tale

west of here between Charlotte and Greensboro. But you got to cross over the Blue Ridge first. Then ask directions from there."

"About how many days ride you think it is?" Johnnie asked.

"Well now, if you don't find trouble, you should make it in six, seven days."

They thanked Mr. Churchill and rode over to the cemetery, where they checked the stones and were relieved there was no sign of one for Jess. Still having most of the day, they rode on.

About twilight, Buford ran up to Doc and Charlie. "Horses coming," he whined.

"Yep," agreed Doc. "Sounds like quite a few, coming fast too."

"Johnnie, I think something's coming. We best get off the road and into those trees over there."

Johnnie didn't question how Charlie knew. He was getting used to the idea that his friend knew lots of things, whether he could just hear better or really did talk to the animals didn't matter. So the little group eased off the road and into some nearby fir trees.

It didn't take long before Johnnie heard horses coming and before they knew it a Reb scouting party galloped by.

"Wait," said Buford. "There's more coming."

Charlie's Tale

Sure enough, coming up fast behind them was a group of Yankee cavalry, a big gun behind them and several wagons filled with troupes.

Charlie and Johnnie waited a while after they all went by and then cautiously returned to the road. The dust hadn't yet settled and Johnnie suggested. "Let's find us a place to bed down. No moon tonight; too dark to keep on. With all this dust, I can't see a thing."

It took another two days of riding before they reached the Blue Ridge and by that time they were running out of food. They hadn't been able to scare up any game either. Johnnie thought it was probably because the soldiers were hunting too. So when they came upon a farm with cotton fields sorely in need of picking, they decided to stop and see if they could exchange some work for food and a bed. A couple of days of rest would be good for them all before they took on the mountains.

The boys rode slowly up to the house with their hands up and visibly empty only to be met by a woman holding a rifle on them, a little girl tugging at her skirt. Both looked thin and ragged.

"What you boys want? I ain't got nothin' left. The other soldiers done took everything."

"Ma'am, my name's Johnnie Stillwell from up around Fredericksburg, Maryland. We're just out looking for our brother, Jess. They say he's probably at Salisbury prison so we're on our way there. But we thought maybe we could

Charlie's Tale

trade some work for some food and a bed. Charlie and me, we could pick your cotton for you."

"Don't have much food for ourselves, but I'd gladly share it for some help with the cotton," she said, lowering her gun. "All the darkies done run off and if'n I don't get that cotton sold, we'll have nothing.

Name's Brady, Mrs. Brady and this is Stella. Go ahead and put your horses up in the back meadow. Some good grass there. I guess the dog can fend for itself. Then come on back here and we'll get some sacks and start picking."

The boys and Mrs. Brady picked cotton until it was just too dark to see. Meanwhile, Stella ran back and forth bringing more sacks and dragging the filled ones back to the barn. They were all dog tired by the time they got back to the house where Mrs. Brady fried up some pork rind to have over biscuits left from the morning. Then they barely made it out to the barn to fall instantly asleep.

The next day they spent picking cotton, not finishing until about eight o'clock that evening.

"We'll be off early tomorrow morning Mrs. Brady. Anything else we can do for you?"

"You boys been a life saver. I'm going to take the cotton over to Norfolk port market tomorrow and me and Stella are going to stay there with my sister until this war is over. There's not much left in the storm cellar, but take what you want. We won't be coming back for a long time, if ever."

Charlie's Tale

In the morning Johnnie and Charlie found a couple of jars of fruit and a small bag of corn meal in the cellar. They packed their saddle bags with the food, mounted up, called to Buford and were off up the hills and into the mountains.

The trail was clear, the weather was good and the Blue Ridge Mountains were beautiful with the late summer flowers. The higher they went the cooler it got and the trees changed to evergreens; pine, spruce and fir. It smelled great.

They didn't see anyone but did see a couple of abandoned cabins along the way. Setting up camp near the top of the ridge, they ate peaches from one of the jars for supper. No fire to be on the safe side.

It took two more days working their way through the mountains. Going down the back side was even harder in some ways because the shale gravel was so slippery. But again, the trails were clear and by the end of the third day they were over and into Kentucky and Charlie had time to think as his horse trotted along.

God, is this part of what I have to learn, the evil of war, the evil of men? I see plenty of good people. What is it that makes people turn to evil things like war? How do we let ourselves get so riled up by something or someone that we are ready to kill? Aren't we smart enough and civilized enough yet to do as You have taught us? And there's the problem that what one group of people thinks is evil is just fine with some other folk.

How can that be?

Charlie's Tale

Kentucky and North Carolina looked much worse than Virginia. Here fields, homes and barns were burnt to the ground. The dispossessed were clogging the roads heading north and east with army units trying to make their way south and west. Charlie and Johnnie stopped a couple of times to ask directions and were told to keep heading south to Greensboro where they could get more directions.

For safety they slept along the side of the road with other travelers and shared what little food they had. The stories of homes lost and family members killed was very hard to hear. They were thankful their farm hadn't been hit, at least as far as they knew.

I can't imagine going through this with my family, Charlie thought. *We wouldn't be at all prepared. How would we stand up to such tragedy?*

Back on the road, thinking about what they were seeing, Charlie said, "Boy, Johnnie, before we got started, I didn't suspect how really bad off the land and the people down here would be. Everything looks dead. Going to take a long time to bring it all back to being useful again."

"Yeah," Johnnie answered, "I'm glad our farm has been spared."

After another day of hard riding, they came to Greensboro, North Carolina, the Guilford County Seat. It was built around a central square with a big courthouse on one side. Cotton was the main industry of the area, but exporting had been pretty much shut down by the Yankee naval blockade

Charlie's Tale

along the east coast. The blockade had also caused food and material shortages, but the town itself was otherwise pretty much untouched by the war.

The boys asked several townspeople which would be the best way to get to Salisbury and about how long it might take. They were told it would take another day to a day and a half to get to the prison.

"We got to find us some food, Charlie. I'm right hungry," Johnnie grumbled. We ain't had anything since that jar of peaches."

"Yeah, my stomach is sure getting loud," Charlie replied.

Heading into a local stable where they put up the horses, they discussed the food possibilities with the hostler.

"You might find some food at one or two of the churches in town," he told them. They're trying to help travelers, especially the ladies of the Women's Benevolent Society at the Alamance Church."

Buford followed the boys around town as they tried to decide who to approach. It was Buford who stopped by an open window of the Alamance Presbyterian Church, Est. 1762.

"This place smells very interesting" he told Charlie. Sure enough there was the smell of food wafting through the window. Looking at each other, all three made a dash for the main door. Buford getting in first.

Charlie's Tale

Inside the small brick church, they followed the sweet smell of food to a kitchen behind the main room. There, an older lady was stirring a large pot on a wood stove.

Johnnie took off his hat. "Excuse me, ma'am. We're looking for someplace we can get a bite of food. Be glad to do some work for you in return for a meal. Name's Johnnie Stillwell and this here is Charlie Richardson."

"You boys do look a might peaked. I'm Ida Blake and if'n you don't mind a bowl of thin soup and some biscuits, we could use some new shingles up on the roof."

"That'll do just fine, ma'am," answered Charlie.

While she was ladling soup into a couple of bowls and giving Buford a bone, she asked where they were from and where they were going. Johnnie explained about trying to find his brother and that they were on their way to Salisbury to see if he had been taken prisoner.

"I hear that's not a very nice place" Ida told them. "Lots of talk about the bad conditions in that prison. Course, most people would say the Yankees deserve it. They don't understand the northerners might be doing the same to our boys. Our church believes in helping everyone in need."

"When y'all are finished with your soup, you'll find some wood shakes out back and a ladder. It'll probably take you the rest of the day, so you can bed down here in the kitchen tonight."

"Thank you, ma'am. We'll do a good job for you."

Charlie's Tale

Mrs. Blake nodded, put her shawl around her shoulders and left the church. Charlie and Johnnie worked on the roof the rest of that day. Buford decided to get into the act, too. He chewed his way through several shakes. Good for the teeth, don't you know.

When the work was finished, they came back to the kitchen and found that Mrs. Blake had left them some more soup and biscuits. She had also laid out a bag of coffee, a bag of corn meal and some jerky with a note for them to take the food and good luck finding Jess.

Charlie thought about Mrs. Blake and the other good people they had met on their travels.

I keep thinking people can be good, so why do they choose to act so bad sometimes?

Men even do evil closer to home; beating up on their wives and kids when they get drunk, cheating or stealing from friends or business clients. It's so different from one place to another though. In some places they kill little girls because they want to have more boys. In other places they treat their wives like cattle. And, there are still places in the world where men, women and children are kept as slaves. What can we do about these things?

* * *

Off again the next morning, moving slowly through green, rolling hills and valleys and gentle streams, they rode south toward Salisbury, and by the end of the seventh day on the road, were able to see the town and the prison from the top of

Charlie's Tale

a nearby hill. The prison stretched out beside the town for about sixteen acres. There were several buildings and many tents surrounded by a stockade wall with two double gates.

Deciding to approach the prison first thing in the morning they made camp in a small copse of pine on the downward slope of the hill.

The following morning they rode slowly around the prison trying to get a feel for the whole thing. There were two guards on the outside gates, then an interior space and two more guards on the interior gates. A stream flowed down from the hills right through the prison and out the other side. There was only one guard tower on the stockade wall with a guard standing duty.

"Stinks, don't it," Johnnie commented.
"Yeah, sure doesn't smell like flowers."

Johnnie dismounted and went up to one of the guards at the gate. "Excuse me; we think our brother might be here. How do we find out? And will we be able to talk to him if he is here?"

"You'll have to see the Commandant. He keeps the roster, but he's away for a couple of days. If you get permission you're allowed to talk with the prisoners in the space between the two gates. Got to leave any guns and knives outside with your horses though. You boys Yankees?"

"No, we're from western Maryland."

Charlie's Tale

"Well, you'll have to wait for the commandant. If'n your brother's here, you can bring him food and clothes if you got some."

"You hear that, Charlie?" Johnnie said, walking back to his horse. "I don't like the idea of waiting around here till the Commandant gets back."

"Me neither. But, let's see what ole Buford can find. Buford, boy, go find Jess."

Buford took off, running along the outside of the stockade, stopping every once in a while to get a whiff of the smells emanating from inside and baying every so often. Charlie and Johnnie tagged along behind, watching and listening.

All at once, Buford stopped and started whining and scratching at a place in the stockade wall. The boys got off their horses and walked up to him. "What is it Buford? Is Jess around here?"

A familiar voice called, "Johnnie, is that you? What are you doing here?"

"Jess? Yeah it's me. You OK"

"I'm OK for now, but this place is real bad. Everybody's got dysentery or typhoid or infected wounds. I got to get out of here soon or I won't make it. There's hardly any food and what we do get is full of maggots. Water's bad too."

"How'd you know it was us, Jess?"

Charlie's Tale

"Why, I'd know ole Buford's voice anywhere," Jess laughed, weakly.

"You got any ideas about getting out? I got a friend with me who's been helping us out at the farm. Name's Charlie. What can we do?"

"I been thinking on it. Since I'm still pretty healthy, they put me with some other guys every morning to go out for some clean water up stream. If you can make some kind of a ruckus, maybe I could slip away into the woods. We might could get away. They don't have too many guards stationed here so they'd be hard pressed to follow."

"OK, we'll think up something. Keep an eye out for us and try to get close to the woods. We'll have the horses hid there."

"How's Ma and Pa and the farm? Everything all right?"

"Everything's fine, but we need you for the harvest."

"All right. See you tomorrow. We go just after first light. I best get on now afore they spot me."

"See you tomorrow, Jess."

Charlie and Johnnie mounted up and rode off toward a large wooded area. "You got any ideas, Charlie?"

"Yeah, I'm thinking we can use Buford to tease up some fun with that work detail while we hide out in the bushes. When you see Jess slip away, give a whistle so he knows where we

Charlie's Tale

are and then we ride like the devil out of here. Buford will follow us. We don't have to worry about him."

"Good idea. I think our best bet is to high tail it into the mountains. It'll be harder for them to chase us up there."

"You're right, but I wish we could come up with another horse for Jess."

"Ain't likely. The armies have took every spare horse and mule for miles around."

They moved their camp into the woods and were up well before dawn, picking their way into a stand of trees and bushes where they couldn't be seen from the stream. While Johnnie was keeping an eye on the gates, Charlie had a talk with the animals. "You guys have to keep real quiet," he told the horses. "We can't let them soldiers know we're here. And Buford, we need you to go on up to the soldiers and get them to play. Make them chase you around but don't get them mad enough to shoot you, hear?"

"We got you, Charlie," answered Doc. "Quiet it is and then we run hard when Jess gets here."

"This is going to be fun," said Buford. "And I'm going to get Jess back."

Just then, the front gate opened and a detail of five prisoners, a wagon filled with empty water kegs and two guards marched out and followed the stream up toward the woods. The men started by getting drinks for themselves and washing up a bit.

"Go on now, Buford. Do your stuff," urged Charlie.

Charlie's Tale

Buford ran into the field and jumped up on the nearest man, pushing him down, straddling him and washing his face with a big sloppy tongue. Then he was off running from one man to another pulling on pant legs, jumping on everyone and finally pushing one of the guards into the water, where he fell, laughing uproariously.

"Catch that danged dog," the other guard shouted, and everyone began chasing Buford from one man to another and in and out of the water until everyone was soaked to the skin and laughing so hard, they forgot who was a prisoner and who was a guard.

Jess gradually eased himself behind a couple of bushes and then quickly crawled deeper into the woods. Johnnie gave a low whistle and Jess ran to meet the boys. He jumped up, behind Johnnie on Doc and they were off running. Buford kept on playing with the men for a while and then took off on the scent of Jess and the horses. They never found out how long it took the guards to figure out Jess was missing. And as far as they could tell, no one followed.

By nightfall, they were well into the mountains, making camp without a fire, eating cold jerky and talking to Jess about the war and prison life.

"So Jess, tell us about the war. Were you in any fights? Did you kill anyone?" Johnnie asked enthusiastically rubbing his hands together.

"Oh, I was in a couple of fights all right. I was with McClellan at Sharpsburg. We had us a mighty big fight with

Charlie's Tale

Lee at Antietam Creek. I swear, I never saw anything like it and I hope I never will again. It started the morning of September 17."

"Them Rebs was fighting like there was no tomorrow and we knew if they won, the States would likely be split up into two countries and we didn't want that to happen. So we gave 'em back about as good as we got. Bullets was whacking against tree trunks every which way and cracking skulls like they was egg shells."

"There was this big fight over a small dirt road, sunken down between two fields. Men caught on that road were slaughtered like animals. And every time I turned around, there was another general with more troupes coming from another direction, both the Rebs and us. I looked to see if Matt was anywhere, but there was too much smoke and I could barely see the fella next to me. Then he got his head shot off and the blood splattered all over me. Got in my eyes and by the time I got that wiped out the fellow on my other side got kilt. I swear, never saw so much blood and guts."

"The nights of the 18th and 19th, Lee finally took his army south across the Potomac and slipped away. We was all rarin' to go after, but McClellan, he just let 'em go. He's not much of a one to go after a fight."

"The next day was even worse though. Everybody who wasn't killed or shot had burial detail. It was a terrible, horrible thing. Men with heads blown off, legs and arms blown away, stomachs tore open with the guts spilling out,

Charlie's Tale

and a million flies everywhere. I'll never forget the smell of putrefying flesh."

"Caps, hats, clothes, canteens, knapsacks, shells, empty casings and dead men scattered wherever you looked over about ten acres. The people living round about made hospitals out of their houses and barns, taking care of the wounded as best they could." He stopped speaking and sighed. "I tell you boys, don't ever ask me to talk about it again."

Johnnie hung his head, ashamed. Charlie, of course, had studied about the Civil War in school, but this first hand account was something else again.

Jess lay down to sleep with Buford snuggled up against him and Johnnie finally said good night. But Charlie had a lot to think about and sat looking up at the stars, his back against an old fir tree.

I know there are people who have big egos; people who just want power. And then, there are people who just have sick minds. But why do the rest of us follow them without thinking for ourselves? And it seems the organized religions don't help. A lot of times they're the cause of war and persecution in the first place. What's with that?
God, what is real evil and what is real goodness?

Charlie's head was buzzing with questions. But finally his eyes closed and he slipped down to the ground and slept until Buford woke him in the morning licking his face.
Discussing things after a breakfast of coffee and biscuits, they decided that Jess would take one horse and head home.

Charlie's Tale

Buford would likely follow him. Johnnie and Charlie would ride double on Doc and head back northeast to Richmond to try to find out from the Confederate headquarters where Matt might be found.

Charlie's Tale

Charlie's Tale

CHAPTER 7

Fall 1863

Jess had no trouble on his way home and was met with open arms by his mom and dad. Mrs. Stillwell did everything she possibly could to fatten him up, insisting he eat everything she put in front of him. Jess didn't mind, he knew it was love and worry that was pushing her so he did his part by eating it all, while Buford sat content against his feet.

Meanwhile, Charlie and Johnnie headed east toward the Confederate capital in Richmond. They had to be careful because skirmishes were still being fought here and there and wild, undisciplined, unattached groups of soldiers were everywhere.

All the past summer there had been fighting around Fredericksburg, Harpers Ferry and the big battle at Antietam Creek in September. And there were still fights going on all up and down the Shenandoah Valley, though, by this time the heavy fighting had moved further south into Tennessee and the Carolinas.

Riding double, it took the boys six days to get to Richmond, where they asked for the Adjutant's office, having learned from their experience in Washington that this would be the most likely place to get information.

Charlie's Tale

Directed to a large, brick house, they discovered a disorganized mess of troupes, officers and private people quarrelling and fighting to get information from a young private who didn't seem to know how to go about finding the answers.

Johnnie turned to Charlie. "This ain't getting' us nowhere, Charlie. Let's see if we can find somebody with some answers."

Walking back outside, they stopped an officer and asked if he knew where General Jackson's Brigade was to be found. "Well now boys, General Jackson and his troupes were in the big battle at Appomattox and then moved on to the battle at Chancellorsville. Jackson was wounded there and died last May.

"After that, General Lee had to reorganize his army and Jackson's brigade was split up between Generals Ewell, Hill and Longstreet. I think you should go on back to the Adjutant's office and ask the clerk to look in the books of those divisions. He should be able to find your brother's name there."

They thanked the major, went back inside and this time spoke directly with the adjutant, a harried lieutenant with carrot red hair and a dirty, torn uniform, who told them to take a seat and he would get to them eventually.

Hours later, the lieutenant looked over and asked for their brother's name and where he had joined up. With this information, he poured over ledger after ledger, interrupted

Charlie's Tale

constantly by soldiers running in and out with messages. Finally, he looked up and told the boys that Matt had been wounded at Appomattox and if he was still alive, could probably be found at one of the hospitals around Washington, D.C.

* * *

Johnnie and Charlie stayed a couple of days in Richmond to rest Doc and get some food. Before they headed back toward Washington, Johnnie snuck into the mess tent one night and stole a package of corn meal and another of coffee and some stale bread. No one would sell, give or lend them another horse. They were too precious and hard to come by, so it was double on old Doc again.

Charlie had a little chat with the horse before they left. "You okay, Doc? I'm sorry to load you up so."

"Long as we take it easy and don't rush, Charlie, I'm just fine," Doc replied.

This time they traveled along the Rappahannock and Potomac rivers and had easier going around the mountains. By now, they were experienced at keeping alert for trouble and hiding out when they heard it coming. But everything was quiet.

Arriving again in Washington, Johnnie and Charlie went directly to the War Department, where they found out the names and locations of the several hospitals around the city. No one could tell them if or where Matt might be

Charlie's Tale

hospitalized. They would have to visit each place and wander through looking for him.

Approaching Saint Elizabeth Insane Asylum, one of the buildings converted into a war hospital, their first sight was an ugly pile of human legs, arms and other body parts, lying in a heap outside the surgery, all bloody, black and swelling with the heat and flies. Next, there was a line of stretchers with bodies covered by gray blankets. Johnnie started turning green but Charlie led him away and they walked on into the hospital.

These hospitals were supposedly better than the ones in the field which were no more than tents, with bare, dirt floors and a long trough dug down the middle where a fire was built to warm the place in the cold weather. These hospitals at least had floors.

Not having found Matt at Saint Elizabeth, Miss Lydia English's Female Seminary, Mount Pleasant and Judiciary Square hospitals, they came at last to the Armory Square Pavilion.

The Armory Square Pavilion was on 7th Street. It consisted of eleven barracks, each 149'x25'. Cots were laid out on each side of the room along the longer walls. Each building held 50 beds and had a section in the rear for a dining room and lodging for the female nurses. At the opposite end were the ward master's room, the bathroom and the water closet.

Johnnie and Charlie walked through each ward. The smell here, like all the hospitals, was vile, putrid. The moans and

Charlie's Tale

cries intermingled with talking and praying by friends and relations around the beds was heart rending.

Charlie had never met Matt, of course, so he couldn't help Johnnie very much, but he stopped to give a drink of water or a helping hand to some of the wounded soldiers. He spoke to the men and tried to reassure each one.

"These hospitals have absolutely no idea of the need for sanitation and basic cleanliness, much less modern equipment for treating these men. Amputation seems to be their only choice for saving a soldier with a wounded limb. The men with body or head wounds have almost no chance of surviving. So many are dying of blood poisoning, tetanus, and gangrene and half the army has Typhus," thought Charlie.

The boys were halfway through the third pavilion at Armory and Charlie could see Johnnie was getting worried they would never find Matt, when suddenly, Johnnie called out excitedly, "Matt, Matt, you're alive."

Matt had been dozing, but his eyes sprang open and a smile lit his haggard face. "Johnnie boy, am I glad to see you." The two brothers awkwardly hugged each other; Matt's right shoulder was heavily bandaged.

Johnnie introduced Charlie and the boys spent the next few hours catching up. Johnnie and Charlie told Matt about their adventures and how they had helped Jess escape from the Reb prison, and Matt talked about his exploits in the army.

"Well, sir, I came through Sharpsburg and a couple of us were billeted at some farmer's house, sleeping in the barn loft. We

Charlie's Tale

still had watch duty every day and I was making my way down the road toward my station when all of a sudden a wild group of raggedy Rebs galloped right into me shooting up a storm. They got me in the shoulder and I fell into a ditch, side the road. Must of thought I was dead, cause they didn't stop, just road on like bats out of hell.

"Took a while for my buddies to find me. By that time I had lost a lot of blood and was near dead. They took me to surgery and took the bullet out. Didn't have anything to put me to sleep with and it hurt like blazes till I finally passed out, but at least they didn't take my arm off."

"Matt, can I take a look at your wound" Charlie asked.

"I know it don't look so good. Don't feel so good either, but go ahead and look."

Charlie took off the bandage. The wound looked bad, beginning to fill with puss. Thinking about it for a while, Charlie told Johnnie he was going out to get some medicine. Outside the tent, he spotted a mess hall where he thought he might have the best chance of finding what he was looking for. Charlie wasn't a doctor by any means, but he remembered the Penicillin his high school chemistry class had grown. He walked over to the mess hall and found some bread with blue mold all over it. Taking what he needed, he returned to Matt's bedside.

"Matt, I've got something here my mom always used for real bad cuts and sores. Is it alright if I put some on your wound?"

Charlie's Tale

"I'll try anything, Charlie. Go ahead."

Charlie removed the old bandage, washed the wound and applied the moss mold he had found. Then he wrapped the wound in a clean bandage, satisfied for the time being, that he had done all he could for Matt.

"Thanks Charlie. Feels better already. Oh, say boys, I want you all to meet my friend next door. Billy, you awake?"

"I'm still here, Matt, thank the Lord. I see you got family with you now."

"Yeah, Johnnie here is my youngest brother and this here is our friend, Charlie."

"How do, Billy," Johnnie said, shaking Billy's hand. At the same time he saw that Billy's left arm had been amputated above the elbow.

"Anything I can do for you," asked Charlie?

"Nope, I'm okay for now. My folks will be by soon. They came down from Philly to tend me."

"And they've been right good to me too," Matt explained. "His mom makes the greatest chicken soup. She says it's an old Jewish recipe to treat the sick."

Charlie nodded to the boys. "Well, I'm going to let you all talk while I walk around some and see if I can help any of the other men in here. Johnnie, you need anything, just call."

Charlie's Tale

Charlie started going from bed to bed talking to the men and tending to their needs as best he could. By the time he got around to Billy again, his folks were at his bedside. His father was praying, rocking back and forth with the rhythm of the prayer, and his mother was spoon feeding Billie with soup.

Billy called Charlie over to meet his folks. "Charlie, this is my mom and dad, Mr. and Mrs. Miller. This is Matt's friend, Charlie," he said between mouthfuls of soup.

Mrs. Miller was a little woman with a beautiful smile. She wore a long dress and a shawl over her head. Mr. Miller was dressed in a black suit and black hat with curls coming down past his ears from under his hat. Some kind of white garment with strings hanging at the four corners was visible under his black vest.

"How do", Charlie said, shaking hands with both parents. "May I ask, sir, what prayer you're reading?"

"Certainly, Mr. Miller replied. This is a prayer from the Old Testament to ask the Lord to heal the sick. Then we'll recite some of the psalms."

"I don't know much about the Jewish religion, sir, except that Jesus was a Jew. Maybe if you have a chance could you explain the differences to me?"

"After our prayers," Mr. Miller replied, "I would be pleased to have a discussion with you."

Charlie's Tale

Sure enough, later that afternoon, Mr. Miller asked Charlie to bring a chair over so they could talk. "First of all, of what religious persuasion are you, Charlie?"

"We went to the Methodist Church back home. But I wasn't ever very serious about religion. Oh, I believe in God. I just never paid much attention in church. Now Johnnie, here, he and his family are Baptist. They go to church every Sunday and his dad reads the Bible to the family Sunday afternoons. They're pretty religions folks. I came to live with them after my folks died in the flu epidemic."

"It is too bad about your parents yet, it seems to me there is something more about you, young man, something more complicated than your parents dying. But, let's leave that for a while," Mr. Miller said, stroking his beard.

"You say the only thing you know about Judaism is that Jesus was a Jew. Is that right?"

"Yes, sir. But Jews don't accept that Jesus was our savior. Why not?"

"You are correct. Most of the Jewish people believe that if there was a man called Jesus, he was probably a prophet like Jeremiah or Ezekiel. There is no real evidence to tell us the truth. We believe that when the Messiah comes there will be no more war; there will be food for everyone and the souls of the righteous will live again. Since that hasn't happened, we believe the Messiah is still to come."

"Okay, but what does the Jewish religion believe in?"

Charlie's Tale

"We believe there is only one God and that we should honor Him and his commandments. We believe that everything in life is holy and we should treat everything with respect and in an appropriate way."

"How do you know the appropriate way?"

"The Torah, the old testament, is our instruction book along with the commentaries of our teachers and sages. Our rabbis are teachers, not religious powers. We believe only in God's power; that He created the universe and continues to be concerned with its governance."

"That's beautiful Charlie smiled, very like the thinking of some, uh other people I've met recently. But what about good and evil?"

"In Judaism, everything we do, everything we touch is holy."

"Therefore if we do harm we have sinned and God may not forgive until He is satisfied that we truly regret our sin, that we have done good deeds in this life to make up for our evil ways. And still we will meet our punishment right here on earth and perhaps in heaven as well."

"We do not believe that we can be redeemed simply by confession, but prayer and good deeds will help."

"Sounds pretty hard to be a Jew. Don't you ever stray from the right path?"

"Of course, but God understands that we are but human. He has given us free will so we can learn and choose the right path. You see, Charlie, Jews do not believe that life is preordained. We believe that God is concerned about us and will show us the way if we ask Him."

"And remember, Charlie, Judaism, Christianity and Islam all believe in the Ten Commandments, even if they might be stated a little differently. Do you remember them?"

"I guess not all of them."

"Let's try to say them together. They tell us how a person should live his life.

1. I am the Lord thy God, which brought thee out of the land of Egypt, from the house of bondage. Thou shalt have no other gods before me.

2. Thou shalt not make unto thee any graven image or any likeness of anything that is in heaven above, or that is in the earth beneath, or that is in the water under the Earth.

3. Thou shalt not take the name of the Lord thy God in vain: for the Lord will not hold him guiltless that taketh his name in vain.

4. Remember the Sabbath day, to keep it holy. Six days shalt thou labor, and do all thy work, but the seventh day is the Sabbath of the Lord thy God: in it Thou shalt not do any work, thou, nor thy son, nor thy daughter, thy man servant, nor thy maidservant, nor thy cattle, nor thy stranger that is within thy gates. For in six days the Lord made heaven and earth, the sea, and all that in them is, and rested the seventh day;

wherefore the Lord blessed the Sabbath day, and hallowed it.

5. Honor they father and thy mother: that thy days may be long upon the land which the Lord thy God giveth thee.
6. Thou shalt not kill.
7. Thou shalt not commit adultery.
8. Thou shalt not steal.
9. Thou shalt not bear false witness against thy neighbor.
10. Thou shalt not covet thy neighbor's house, thou shalt not covet thy neighbor's wife, nor his manservant, nor his maidservant, nor his ox, nor his ass, nor any thing that is they neighbor's. "

"You see, Charlie, the first five commandments refer to God and man and the second five are about man personally."

"The Old Testament is part of our Bible too, Mr. Miller, but then it picks up with Jesus' life and death and the testaments of the Apostles," Charlie said.

"But, thank you Mr. Miller. I understand a little better now. Can we continue talking when you come to visit again?"

"Certainly, Charlie. But, now tell me, God has put you here to learn, yes?"

"Yes, sir. I have a lot to learn."

Charlie's Tale

"And your spirit will continue to grow. Yes, I see that now," whispered Mr. Miller.

Then, he placed a hand on Charlie's head and blessed him then Johnnie and Matt.

Just then, Mrs. Miller came around the beds with some hot soup. "I've made enough for all of you", she said. "Eat while it's hot." The boys dug in relishing the wonderful taste after all the stale bread and jerky they had been eating.

* * *

Either Charlie's medicine or the chicken soup seemed to be helping Matt, and while they waited for him to heal enough to be released from the hospital, Johnnie and Charlie spent their time helping the other men in the ward. Many needed their dressings changed or wanted help writing home to let their families know where they were or that they would soon be home. But Charlie knew the list of the dead would be a long one. He tried to reassure them, held their hands and spoke quietly to those who lay dying.

Every time the Miller's came to visit, the boys joined them in prayer, until finally one day Matt and Billy were well enough to go home.

There was no way Matt would be able to ride a horse, so they would have to find some kind of wagon that could carry him. Johnnie and Charlie asked around town at the churches and hospitals and the various stables, but what was available was for sale and they had no money.

Charlie's Tale

Mr. Miller had also been asking the people in the Jewish community around Washington and he rushed in one morning with the perfect solution. One of his acquaintances was going to take a trip to visit a congregation in Pittsburgh. He would be glad to have company and they could make Matt comfortable in the back of his buckboard.

"This is our chance, Johnnie. There's room for all of us and Doc can help pull the wagon."

"Yep and I'll telegraph Pa to meet us in Hagerstown," Johnnie agreed. "That'll put us just south of the Pennsylvania line and near to the farm."

A mess sergeant gave them some sacks of food and Charlie got a supply of clean bandages and a crutch from one of the doctors.

A couple of days later a rather thin young man with a black beard, dressed in a long, black coat and a big brimmed, black hat suddenly appeared at Matt's bedside with Mr. Miller.

"Gentleman, announced Mr. Miller, this is your ride to Pittsburgh. Meet Yehuda Levi." They all shook hands and then proceeded to carry Matt outside to the buckboard. Matt waved a final farewell to Billy and his folks and before he knew it, was tucked into a bunch of blankets, attended by Johnnie, three barrels of potatoes, two barrels of apples and a crate of chickens.

Charlie's Tale

Charlie introduced himself to Strawberry, Yehuda's horse, who proceeded to welcome Doc and then he got up on the front seat with Yehuda.

"Nice horse," he told Yehuda. "Strawberry looks to be in really good shape."

"Your horse looks good and fit too," he replied.

"Yeah, old Doc is a great one. Knows the score too."

"You talk funny, Charlie."

"Just where I come from, Yehuda."

"Well animals are also God's creatures, so it's our obligation to take good care of them, right?"
"Right. Say Yehuda, why are you going to Pittsburg?"

"I'm delivering a candelabra which we call a menorah, to a new congregation there. It arrived in Baltimore harbor several weeks ago, but it has taken me some time to arrange for this trip."

Yehuda clucked to the horses and they were off, headed northwest.

Charlie's Tale

Charlie's Tale

CHAPTER 8

It took all day to get out of the Washington area and into the countryside. It was October, and the weather had turned cool. The nights were actually cold, so as evening fell, they stopped at a road house and slept in the barn so Matt could be kept out of the night air. Bundled between the hay bales, they slept comfortably until morning. After something to eat, they were off again heading north, through western Maryland.

By now the leaves had fallen from the trees and were blowing about in swirls by a cold wind. The sun looked weak and pale in the sky. The farm land, either burnt or harvested, lay barren around them; old corn stalks sticking up out of the ground like skeletons.

Toward afternoon, Charlie took over the driving so Yehuda could relax for a while. It was easy going, the weather was good and they were on one of the few main roads out of Washington heading toward western Pennsylvania.

As the horses plodded along, Yehuda snoozed gently, his head bobbing with the movement of the wagon. Johnnie and Matt talked quietly about their plans for the farm and Charlie was day dreaming when suddenly, bursting out of the trees up onto the road, came three riders in tattered Union uniforms. As the startled horses broke into a run, Yehuda almost fell off

Charlie's Tale

his seat. Charlie had all he could do to get control of the horses.

The three riders galloped after them, shooting and shouting for them to stop. Charlie knew he couldn't out run the men with their loaded wagon so when he finally got control of the horses, he pulled to a stop. The riders rode up, their guns drawn.

"What ya got there mister? Any liquor?"

"We don't have anything but a wounded soldier and some food, Charlie answered. If'n you're hungry, we could spare you some."

"Bobby, get down and take a look up there," the leader ordered.

One of the men got off his horse and climbed up onto the wagon where he started pulling things about until he uncovered the silver menorah.

"Well look a here, Joe. I reckon we could get us some money for this thing."

"That is a sacred religious piece," shouted Yehuda. "You cannot have it. I am to deliver it to people in Pittsburgh."

"Oh, are you now," Joe answered. "Well it ain't any part of my religion. I bet we could melt her down to a nice silver bar. Right fellas," he laughed.

Yehuda started to grab for the menorah, but Charlie pulled him back, as Joe and the third man cocked their guns.

Charlie's Tale

"Now just take it easy fellas," Charlie suggested quietly. "Nobody needs to get hurt here. Go on take the thing and leave us be."

"No," Yehuda shouted, about to jump up again, but Charlie shook his head and looked hard at him. Yehuda eased back down. He realized Charlie had something in mind.

Bobby, lifted the menorah and was about to get off the wagon when Charlie said something softly to the horses. They both jumped ahead. Bobby fell to the floor of the wagon. Matt drew a gun out from under his blanket and shot at the three thieves. He got the leader, Joe in the left shoulder. Then, a huge rock came flying out of nowhere and knocked the third man off his horse, where he lay unconscious. The wagon jerked forward and sped away, Bobby rolling out to land in a ditch.

After a bit, Charlie eased the horses to a walk, looking back to make sure they weren't being followed.

"They're not coming," Johnnie called out. "I think we're rid of 'em Charlie."

"Well let's keep our eyes open boys. We're in some pretty rough country in some pretty rough times," Charlie cautioned.

"Where the heck did that big rock come from?" Matt asked.

"I have no idea," Charlie laughed. That was a long throw, even for his friend, Muffin.

Charlie's Tale

They had no more trouble on the rest of the trip and by late morning of the 4th day, they pulled into Hagerstown where they stopped at the local livery to ask directions. They were told that Yehuda's contact ran the local suttler's shop and Mr. Stillwell was already in town. In fact, his horse and wagon were stabled right there. The livery man suggested they look for him at the Cap & Pub.

Yehuda drove over to the pub and sure enough, Johnnie spotted Mr. Stillwell sitting inside at a table talking with the publican.

"Pa," Johnnie called from the doorway. "Come on out here. We got us a wounded soldier for you to take a look at."

Mr. Stillwell, grinning hugely, got up and made his way outside to the wagon. He looked Matt over and hugged him tightly. Then putting an arm around Johnnie and Charlie, said, "Thank you boys. You did good."

The three helped Matt out of the wagon and onto a nearby bench. "Many thanks, sir," Mr. Stillwell said to Yehuda, shaking his hand." If there is anything my family can ever do for you, just let us know."

Yehuda thanked him, said his farewells to the boys and pulled away to go deliver the menorah to his friends.

Johnnie went off to get his Pa's wagon and after gently laying Matt on some blankets in the back, they all piled in and headed out to the farm. On the way, the three boys filled Mr. Stillwell in on everything that had happened to them. Matt

Charlie's Tale

told about the war and how he had been shot. Johnnie and Charlie talked about the people they had met and how impressed they had been with the buildings in Washington.

The reunion when they got home was something to behold. Buford was the first to hear them coming and set to howling up a storm. As the wagon pulled to a stop, Ma Stillwell came running out of the house and Jess from out of the barn, pitchfork in hand. They were all over Matt with hugs and kisses until Ma Stillwell finally suggested they get him settled in the house.

"Matt took in a deep breath as they helped him into the house and into the old rocker. "Oh, man, Ma, it sure smells good in here. What's for dinner?"

"I thought you'd all be coming along about now and would probably be starving for some good food. So, Jess shot us a goose and, of course, its apple pie time."

Jess pulled a jug of cider out of the cool box. "Set yourselves down and have a pull, he said as he handed the jug to Matt, who took a drink and passed it along to the others. Charlie took a swig then just sat back, admiring the family and their obvious love for one another as Ma Stillwell served up a truly delicious meal.

The conversation during dinner was all about the war from both sides and the adventures of Johnnie and Charlie while looking for the brothers.

Charlie's Tale

"Well, where do the armies stand now," Mr. Stillwell wanted to know.

"Lee's not beat yet," Matt replied. "But he's lost a lot of men, not to mention generals. Jackson was a real loss. Food and supplies are real low. Most of 'em don't even have shoes now."

"With Sherman heading southeast and Grant heading east, it can't be long before the end," noted Jess.

"Ole Lee could still have something up his sleeve though," replied Matt. "Say, Pa, how're things goin' with the farm? Were we raided at all? Did you get some planting done?"

"Things have been all right, considering, Matt. We had a few people on the move pass by, but the harvest has been great. For some reason, we had a heap more bees and butterflies around this spring, more than we ever saw before. I think that's what helped along with the good weather. This country's going to need as much food as we can grow seeing as the armies have spoiled so much."

"Well, I hope to be fixed pretty good by next Spring and ready for the planting."

Charlie smiled to himself, thinking about Blue's butterflies and bees. It seemed his friends were keeping an eye on him.

* * *

The family gradually settled down to the routines of the farm again and as Charlie was brushing the horses one morning, not long after they were back, he felt that old pull to leave.

Charlie's Tale

How sad. He liked the Stillwell family and the farm so much. It would be hard to leave. He was thinking about how he would say his goodbyes, when old Doc interrupted his thoughts.

"Yeah, Charlie, I guess they're calling you to move on aren't they? We'll sure miss you around here."

"And I was just getting used to you. You do give a pretty good rubdown," Mule admitted. "Where they goin' to send you now, Charlie?"

"Don't rightly know boys. I'll have to wait till I get back up there to find out. I'll really miss you guys and the family. You be good to them. They'll treat you right. Sam, you old Mule, if that foot starts hurting again, just go up to Johnnie and give him a nudge."

Just then Charlie heard the clang of the iron triangle calling everyone to dinner. He finished his brushing, put the tools away and walked toward the house still thinking about how to tell the Stillwells goodbye.

After saying grace, everyone dug in to fried chicken, corn muffins and boiled cabbage. With their mouths full, no one talked about anything. But as the meal wound down, the talk picked up. Matt was doing better, but still had to rest most of the day. Hopefully he'd be up and ready for spring planting. Jess was going to take his mom into town to trade eggs for a few things at the store and Johnnie and Mr. Stillwell were going to pull down some hay from the barn loft for the stock.

Charlie's Tale

"I guess I'll go with you into town, Jess, Charlie said. I'm going to head out to Indiana. While we were looking around D.C. for Matt, I met a man who said there was a pack of Richardsons around that big lake Michigan. Thought they might be related.

"You folks have been awful good to me, but I'd like to know if I have any people of my own."

Everyone stopped eating and stared at Charlie. "Hey, you can't go, Charlie. You're one of us. I couldn't have found these guys without you," cried Johnnie.

"Charlie, we look at you as part of our family," added Mr. Stillwell. "But, if you really feel like you've got to go, just remember you'll always be welcome back if things don't work out."

"I thank you all. It's really hard to leave. I've been real happy here, but something's just a calling me."

"Yes, I can see that," nodded Ma Stillwell. "Some men have a need to travel. The wilderness calls to them."

The next day, Charlie said his goodbyes and leaped up on to the buckboard.

"Oh, Mr. Stillwell, here are some seeds I found down around Kentucky. They say these grow some really fine millet. Thought you might like to plant some, try it out here," he said, taking a packet out of his pocket and handing it over.

"Thanks, Charlie. We'll do just that."

Charlie's Tale

As they drove off, the sun was rounding up above the far horizon. A mist was rising from the fields and the air was filled with dew. Charlie realized how little he had appreciated these things during his life. Even when he went out hunting, his mind was on the hunt and his equipment, not on the natural world around him. *It's just so nice*, he thought.

Once in town, Charlie said good-by to Jess, hugged Ma Stillwell, and walked off down the road. The next thing he knew, he was floating through the sky, heading toward Meg's bright light.

PART 3

CHAPTER 9

"Hey, Meg. It's good to see you again. "Hi Charlie. It's good to see you too"

"It looks like you were just sitting on that little cloud waiting for me. Did you get all those new souls from the exploding planet taken care of?"

"Most of them are all set and I wasn't needed anymore. Besides, I wanted to see how you were doing. Pull up a cloud and tell me about your experience this time? I can't wait to hear all about your trip."

Charlie looked around and found a misty cloud to sit on.

"The Stillwell's were wonderful people, Meg. I wouldn't have minded staying there forever. They were a real family, working together, helping each other and showing their concern for each other. It was really hard when the family made different choices during the war. Matt and Josh could have killed one another, and their parents knew that."

"These trips have really got me thinking. I could have made my family like the Stillwell's. I just didn't think to try.

"What else did you learn, Charlie?"

Charlie's Tale

"Well, you know Meg, I never really thought much about God when I was alive. Oh, sure, I went to church and knew about the Ten Commandments, Jesus and all, and we celebrated some of the holidays. But, when you see, really see, the beauty of the world and then you see all the evil caused by man, you can't help but wonder. What is God doing? Why are some people bad? Why is something that's considered wrong in some countries, considered okay in others, like slavery? Why do a lot of bad people seem to do real well while a lot of good people have a terrible struggle all their lives? Why do we inflict such horror on one another and why does God let this happen? I still don't get it," he said shaking his head.

"At least you're beginning to see things differently, Charlie. Unfortunately, we are just human. We can't see God's larger plan and we don't often see the real punishment God has in store for bad people."

"Well, I did learn something about the difference between Judaism and Christianity, Meg. These religions believe in God and know there is good and evil in the world. Some orthodox Christian communities believe that total faith in Jesus will save their souls if they confess and repent their sins to a priest. But, I can't see that. After all, priests are just men. Other denominations are not quite so conservative."

"Now the Jews believe they may be punished for their sins right there on earth as well as in the afterlife. They have to confess directly to God and believe God knows if they are really sorry or not. And, they have to perform good deeds to

Charlie's Tale

make up for their sins. In fact, they're supposed to do a good dead every day anyway."

"What denomination were you, Charlie?"

"We were Methodists, Meg. But like you reminded me, I wasn't much good at it."

"I don't know. I'm very confused. Mom said I was beginning to learn, but the more I see out there, the less I'm sure of."

"Sure you're learning, Charlie. I can see it. You are considering questions about life and good and evil you would not have thought about before and what's more, you wouldn't have cared."

"I guess. If you say so. I just don't feel like I've learned very much, Meg."

"You've made a lot of progress, Charlie and you've been a good person and a good friend on this trip. Remember, you're still learning. Now your next visit is going to be quite different. For one thing, you're going to be a young woman!"

"Don't kid me, Meg. How can I be a woman?"

"Oh, you can be anything, Charlie. Remember men do have an X chromosome. You might find this an interesting change," she smiled.

"Well okay, but I don't know if I can handle being a woman! "Why do I have to be a woman?", he grumbled.

"To give you a whole different perspective, Charlie. I think you'll do just fine."

Charlie's Tale

"So where am I going this time, to be a woman?" Charlie asked sarcastically.

"You're going to China. You'll be in current earth time, the same year you died, but you'll be living in an entirely different society."

"That does sound interesting; I always wanted to travel and now I'm going to places I never dreamed of going.

"Off you go, Charlie. Enjoy yourself and keep learning."

Next thing he knew, Charlie was flying high again. *This flying thing is a breeze. Just lay back and relax and don't worry about what's coming next. After all, so far, so good.*

Charlie's Tale

CHAPTER 10

All of a sudden, Charlie was walking down a dusty road with scrubby, dusty bushes on either side. It was spring time and in the adjacent fields he noticed figures wearing straw hats, bending over, planting crops. He didn't see any machinery. The work was all being done by hand.

"I guess I better stop and take stock of myself. Let's see. I'm a lot shorter and much thinner. My hair is hanging down my back, I've got some kind of pantaloons on with a long shirt, flip-flop shoes, and well, would you look at that, I've got boobs! I'm a woman! This is going to take some getting used to!

Now what's this, a stick with a bundle on the end? Must be my stuff. I'd better take a look. Charlie opened the pack and found a canteen of water, a chunk of stale bread and another shirt. Tucked inside the shirt was a note addressed to Aunt Lieu Woo Ming at a location in Shanghai. *This must be where I'm supposed to go,* he thought. Continuing to look, he found a map of Shanghai written in Chinese. *They think of everything up there. I can even read Chinese.* Shaking his head he began putting everything back in the pack.

"Looks like I'm headed to Shanghai," he said aloud to no one in particular. Throwing the stick with its bundle over his

Charlie's Tale

shoulder, he walked on, secure in the fact that he was headed in the right direction.

For a while, Charlie didn't see any traffic, no moving vehicles of any kind. Then he saw a roadside sign, 'Ten Kilometers to Shanghai'. *I can read that sign too. This is really weird.*

Down the road Charlie noticed a man on a bike. Then, he saw a cart pulled by a horse. A little moped zipped past both and seemed to be headed toward him. Charlie moved over quickly to the side of the road and let the traffic go by. No one said anything to him and he walked on. A little later, he heard a truck coming up from behind.

Hey, maybe I can get a lift. He was about to stick out his thumb, but that didn't seem lady-like, so he waived. The truck pulled to a stop and an elderly man motioned him to get in.

"Shanghai?" he asked. The old man nodded and drove on down the road.

They didn't speak any further as the fields rapidly turned into the squalor, noise and pollution of a huge city. There were people bustling through the streets with every kind of locomotion, bikes, mopeds, motorcycles, cars, rickshaws and feet. The honking horns, bells and whistles were making a huge racket. The streets and sidewalks were jammed with pedestrians and small shops.

"Busy city," Charlie said to the old driver. The old man merely nodded, keeping his eyes on the road.

Charlie's Tale

"So many people. Looks worse than the pictures of New York. And such a racket. I guess they don't have any laws about not blowing your horns here. Everybody's hurrying on some kind of transportation. Quite a few new cars."

The truck pulled onto a main street with high-rise buildings across from a broad plaza and park. Beyond the park was a river crowded with small boats, barges and large ships. And, beyond the river, Charlie could see new, modern buildings under construction. The city seemed to be booming.

Just then, the truck pulled over and stopped. The old man motioned for him to get out. Charlie thanked him and stepped out onto the plaza. The question now was how to find his family. Looking around he spotted a couple of uniformed men strolling along the broad walkway. Guessing they were police, he walked right up and asked them in beautiful Mandarin for directions.

The two officers smiled at the young woman who introduced herself as Charlie. To his amusement, they pronounced the name Char-Lee and Charlie decided that was as good a name as any for his new identity.

Pointing and gesturing, the men discussed the best way for her to get to her destination. Thanking them and waving, Char-Lee walked off down the street. She saw many different kinds of housing; old hovels no more than pig sties with roofs, people living behind or above their shops, and many concrete apartment blocks, obviously built by the communist government in the last fifty years.

Charlie's Tale

Charlie's Tale

"The communists sure built some ugly buildings, Charlie thought. But, I guess, they had to do something to house all these people and I guess they are better than the shacks around them. I forget how many people live in China, but it must be a lot more than America."

Newly washed clothes hung out of almost every window and balcony. Merchants hawked their wares in front of open shop doors. Artisans worked at tables set up in front of their homes and shops. Everyone was busy.

Char-Lee gradually made her way into an older part of the city where narrow streets and ramshackle houses squeezed tightly together. She managed to find the correct street but was standing at the corner, trying to figure out which was the right house when two mangy dogs came up to her. They stopped to sniff around her feet.

"What are you looking for, Spirit," one of them asked.

"Hi, fellas, I'm looking for the Lieu Woo Ming home. Have you got any idea which is their house?"

"That's my family," answered the larger dog. "My name is Ah-Choo. Just come along with me, Spirit. See ya later Mao," Ah-Choo called to his friend as he turned tail and headed down the street.

"Thank you Ah-Choo. My name is Char-Lee. Would you tell me a little about your family? How many people live in your house and what are their names?"

Charlie's Tale

"Well let's see. There is the very old grandmother. Her name is Old Grandmother. Then there are Grandmother, Mother and Father and the child, Jan Ping, a female.

Old Grandmother stays home all day and cooks and prays. She has a strange, strong smell. Grandmother goes to a place where there are smelly clothes and hot water and soap. Mother and Father go to a shop with good smells and sometimes they give me a bone when I visit the shop. The child goes to school every day and comes home as the sun goes down. She smells of lemon."

Ah-Choo turned quickly into a gate in an old wooden fence, up two steps and directly in through the open door of the neat little house. Char Lee saw there were pots of colorful flowers all around the doorway, a front garden and musical chimes hanging from the eaves sang with the breeze. She rapped on the door post and looked around as she waited.

"This looks real nice. Pretty old, but well cared for. The garden looks bigger than the house. I wonder how many rooms there are inside, she mused".

Soon she heard someone moving slowly through the house and a very old lady came to the door. Her grey hair was pulled tightly back into a bun on the back of her head and the wrinkles in her rosy cheeks almost hid the sparkle in her alert brown eyes. She bowed to Char-Lee and smiled, showing many more wrinkles and a toothless mouth.

"Good morning, Old Grandmother. I am Char-Lee. I received a letter inviting me to come live with you after my

Charlie's Tale

parents died in the ferry boat accident. I did not know what I would do until I received the letter from Auntie asking me to become part of your family. I thank you Old Grandmother."

The old woman's smile lit up her whole face. She motioned Char-Lee inside and sat her down at a large table next to a lively fire. Ah-Choo had settled himself nicely on the warm hearth. Moving very slowly, the old lady took a kettle off the fire and filled two cups with hot tea. She placed them one at a time on the table and sat down motioning Char-Lee to drink.

As Char-Lee picked up the cup, she nodded and looking satisfied said in a very soft voice, "You are Char-Lee. Very pretty. So sorry about mother and father. After tea we will pray to Jade Emperor for a good after life for them and rebirth into a better life."

She sighed with satisfaction as she sat back, relaxing over her tea. Char-Lee followed her lead, enjoying the hot tea after the long walk. *"It ain't no cold beer though"*, she thought.

When they were finished with tea, Old Grandmother motioned for Char-Lee to follow her out the back door to a small, covered porch. At one end of the porch was a statue of Buddha. She placed some herbs into a shallow bowl in front of the Buddha and taking a long match from a nearby wicker basket, lit them. This was obviously some kind of incense and Char-Lee realized what Ah-Choo had meant about the old lady's smell.

Charlie's Tale

Putting her hand on Char-Lee's shoulder, she urged her down so that she was kneeling next to her as she began to pray. The old woman was not praying to the Buddha but to one of the old gods she called the Jade Emperor. When she was finished, Char-Lee helped her to her feet and they went back into the kitchen to wait for the family.

"You do not pray to Buddha, Old Grandmother?"

"Oh yes, I do my child. But for certain things it is better to pray to the old gods. You know, do you not, that Jade Empower is the ruler of heaven and knows how to deal with all the other gods of heaven. Jade Emperor created the world and helped Yuan-Shi-Tian-Zong bring order to everything. The Imperial rulers of old China and today's leaders are merely images and servants of the Jade Emperor," she sneered. "They are of no consequence, only let rule by Emperor. His word is law. He rules heaven and earth with the help of his many lower officials."

Just then, Grandmother came in the door, a young girl hanging back behind her.

"And who is this?" Grandmother asked officiously as they took off their shoes.

"I am your great niece," Char-Lee replied, bowing to her.

"Ah, yes. You are welcome, Char-Lee," she sighed. "You will mean another mouth to feed, but, she admitted, also another pair of hands to work." She looked Char-Lee over carefully,

Charlie's Tale

and finally nodding, helped herself to some tea and sat down, sighing again and rubbing her feet together.

This seemed to relieve the girl, who said hello and knelt beside Char-Lee. She was brimming over with questions. Where did I come from? How were we related? Did I have sisters and brothers? Were there more cousins? What did I think of Shanghai? Was I going to go to school or work? Could I read and write? What poetry did I like? Could I play an instrument?

"Enough, enough," Grandmother shouted. There is time to answer everything later, Jan Ping. Char-Lee must be tired after her long journey. She will sleep near you. Show her where to put her sleeping pallet and let her rest until dinner."

Jan Ping chatted up a storm as she took Char-Lee to a small room toward the rear of the house where two sleeping pads were neatly rolled up against a wall. Throwing down her pack, she unrolled one of the pads and plopped down on it.

She was a pretty girl, a gangly pre-teen with long black hair and bangs hanging almost over her eyes. A tiny nose. No nose ring Char-Lee noticed, but absolutely jeans and gym shoes like every other kid Char-Lee knew.

"So tell me," she began, "what is it like where you lived. I'm really sorry about your parents. Did you live in a house? Did you go to school? Can you read and write? What kind of work did your parents do? Do you have any brothers and sisters?"

Charlie's Tale

"Whoa, Jan Ping. You ask too many questions at once. Slow down. First, I have no brothers and sisters. My parents obeyed the one child rule. Yes, I graduated school and can read and write. But now that I am here, I will look for a job. We lived in Hubei Provence, in a house near a big river. One day my parents were sailing across on the ferry to go to the market and the boat sank. There were too many people on board, you see, and my parents were killed, along with many others. Now, I will live with you.

"But, tell me, Jan Ping, what are you studying in school? Do you have a boy friend yet?"

"Oh, no boy friend. I am not yet a woman, but I have lots of girl friends. My favorite class now is English. We have an American lady teaching in China for a year and she is very nice. Sometimes she plays Western music for us if we finish our class early. I am very glad you are here Char-Lee. You will be my sister and I will be yours. Are you a woman yet, Char-Lee?"

"Of course, can't you see that I am a woman?"

"No, I mean are you a woman with your monthly cycle?"

Now that brought me up short. What should I say? Am I going to be a real, complete woman? Good lord! I better check some of the shops and see if I can figure out how Chinese women take care of these things, just in case.

"Uh, Jan Ping, that is not a nice question to ask someone. It is a private matter."

Charlie's Tale

"Oh, yes, sorry to offend Char-Lee."

"I am not offended, but you should not ask others such private things? Now, why don't you show me your garden before dinner. It looks beautiful."

Jan Ping took Char-Lee out to the back yard and pointed out the borders filled with lilies, daisies and alyssum and a separate bed filled with squash, tomatoes, greens and several kinds of herbs. A small fountain surrounded by smooth black stones sat under a weeping cherry tree with a wooden bench nearby. It was a very peaceful place for anyone wanting a private moment.

Soon, we heard voices coming from the house. "Mom and dad are home Char-Lee," Jan Ping crowed. "Come and meet them," She took Char-Lee's hand and pulled her into the house.

Jan Ping was her mother's daughter. LieuWoo Ming had short, black hair curving around a round cheeked face with the same tiny nose and large eyes. She was medium height and slim with energy just popping out of her.

Her husband, Lieu Chan, was taller and slim, but with hefty shoulders and forearms. He looked like he lifted weights.

They both dropped their bags and welcomed Char-Lee to their home. Woo Ming hugged her and then took her aside. "We are so sorry about your parents, Char-Lee. From now on, this will be your home. Have you given thought to what

Charlie's Tale

you will do once you have rested from your trip? Will you go to school or work? Do you have any special training?"

"I have my school certificate, so I will find work, Auntie. I have no special talent, but my mother taught me the use of our sewing machine and I can read and write. Perhaps you can suggest places for me to search for work."

"I will think about this and ask our friends and neighbors. I'm sure we will be able to find you something suitable. Now let us join the family for dinner."

Talk at dinner was about the ordinary things of their lives. How school was going for Jan Ping, Grandmother wanted to know how business was that day and Old Grandmother chastised her daughters for not using cream on their hardworking hands. "I will make some almond butter cream for all of you," she offered.

Dinner began with a simple sweet and sour soup followed by rice and vegetables in a dark soy sauce, then a fish stew in a light sauce that was delicious. Of course, we often had Chinese food at home, but this tasted much better. The rice was dark, almost like whole wheat bread and the vegetables obviously came from the garden. Char-Lee thought the chunks of fish tasted a lot like Cod, but she had never had it in a stew.

The next few days, Char-Lee explored Shanghai; the parks where children played, watched over by their mothers or grannies and where old men sat and played chess and couples danced for exercise. She looked into some of the major

Charlie's Tale

buildings, walked the streets investigating shops and restaurants, and helped Old Grandmother about the house. Working with the old woman gave Char-Lee a chance to talk with her about life when she was young and how the many changes in China had affected her, the family and her beliefs. She was a great store of information.

One afternoon while they were chopping vegetables for dinner, Char-Lee asked about her childhood.

"Born this house, Char-Lee, 1918. Just end of Ch'ing Dynasty and beginning of Republic of China. Republic made official in 1928. Things much different those times. Just over revolution. Sun Yat-sen new leader more interested in how people live, who owned land and educating people.

"Old things starting to be put aside. My mother not bind my feet. Too much happening and changing about that time. I glad not bind feet. Those women very crippled, can barely walk if can walk at all. But I not understand much. I just child"

"What god did your family worship, Old Grandmother?"

"Mother pray to Jade Emperor, Lavatory Lady and Kitchen God, sometimes Buddha. Father pray to Buddha."

"You were going to tell me more about Jade Emperor. Will you tell me now?"

"Ah, Jade Emperor. Jade Emperor is ruler of heaven, creator of universe and lord of imperial court. He start at bottom of court and work hard bringing order to universe until he get to top. For billion years he sit and contemplate navel until he achieve state of most amazingly perfect Grace. Then he become heavenly ruler and Emperor of Universe. Earthly rulers given leave to rule but must use Pi Disc to check in often every so often with Jade Emperor."

"What is a Pi-Disc, Old Grandmother?"

"I do not know, my child. I am too far below rulers to know this."

"One time, people who believe in Daoism and Buddhism make Jade Emperor most holy god. He is master at winning by doing nothing."

"But Old Grandmother, last time you talked about Jade Emperor you said he had a hard time dealing with Monkey. Tell about Monkey God and how he was dealt with."

"That is a story for another time, Char-Lee. Now I will rest and you will weed garden, yes?"

Char-Lee thought about this new information and wondered what effect these stories still had on the younger Chinese population.

* * *

That evening, Woo Ming told Char-Lee about the possibility of a job in a shirt waist factory and she went for an interview the next morning.

The factory was located in an industrial area near the river. It was a large, brick building covered in black soot, standing

Charlie's Tale

among many others of the same ilk. Trucks and vans of all sizes plied the narrow streets and pulled into various size docks to load or unload.

The front door of the factory was locked, so with heart pounding with excitement she rang the bell and a buzzer released the door to open. No one was at the entry desk in the front hall, but a sign directed people to an office on the second floor. Arriving at the top of the stairs, Char-Lee saw a huge room with row upon row of people sitting at sewing machines and large cutting tables presided over by men cutting cloth from patterns. Ironers stood in the back of the room over steaming machines.

The room was hot and steamy even though it had a high ceiling with a big, open skylight and small windows open high up along one wall.

A woman sitting near the stairs looked up from her machine and pointed Char-Lee toward a small office to her left.

The door was open, so she knocked on the door frame. A middle aged gentleman in shirt-sleeves, looked up from the accounting books on his desk, motioned her in and to a chair across from him.

"How do you do, sir. My name is Char-Lee. I understand that you are hiring seamstresses for your factory and I wish to apply for a job."

Charlie's Tale

"How do you do, Miss. I am Mr. Xiang, owner of this establishment. And yes, I am looking for more workers. What experience do you have? Where did you work before?"

"I lived in a small village in Hubei Province near the new Three Dams Project until my parents died. Now, I have come to live with my Aunt Lieu Woo Ming and my Uncle Lieu Chan. I have just completed school and have no work experience, though I did help my mother sew for our village, Mr. Xiang. I learn quickly and I would work very hard," Char-Lee responded.

"I don't usually hire inexperienced people, Miss. But right now, it is hard to find workers. Everyone wants to have their own shop," he said throwing up his hands in despair. The government has become more lenient, that's the trouble. I will give you a trial. Be here at 8:00 tomorrow morning. We work until 6:00 in the evening and one-half hour for lunch. You should be serious about your work. No talking with others, except while you are learning or if you have a problem. You understand?"

"Oh, yes sir. I am quite a serious person."

Down stairs again, Char-Lee decided it would be a good time to stop by her Uncle's shop to see what it was like. She looked at the little map Woo Ming had drawn for her that morning and saw that the store was not too far from their house. But, in order to get there she would have to take a different route from the one she had taken to the factory

Charlie's Tale

because the streets didn't cut all the way through the city from where she was standing.

This route led through a market where food coming into the city by river and truck came for distribution to smaller shops. First she walked through stinking slaughter houses with pens of animals squeezed next to them. Fish stalls were set up next to the docks collecting barrels-full from the incoming boats.

"Boy, I don't know which smells worse, the slaughter houses or the fish stalls. Ouch! Hey, watch where you're going with that crate." A workman had bumped into Char-Lee with a crate of oranges.

"Sorry, sorry, Miss", he bowed as he hurried to the next shop.

Produce, lined up next to the docks and workmen shuffled boxes from boat to pier to market stall. There was a huge variety. All kinds of rice and beans in sacks, green, yellow, orange, red and brown vegetables in bins, apples, pears, grapes, melons, peaches, all looking fresh and beautiful.

"Whoa there." A boy was chasing an orange that had gotten away and almost knocked her down. He grabbed the orange and smiled as he put it back in the crate.

All this food was making Char-Lee hungry. "Excuse me old aunt, how much for an apple she asked an old woman minding a barrel of apples? The old woman had a kerchief tied around her hair and a large dirty apron over her dress and held up three fingers. Char-Lee gave her some of the

Charlie's Tale

spending money Woo Ming had given her and went on, happily munching the fresh apple.

Following the path through the market, she suddenly smelled the wonderful aroma of fresh bread. Around a corner sat tables stacked with fresh loaves made with different kinds of flour. Round loaves, rectangular loaves and a few twisted like a braid, were just being taken with a large wooden paddle out of a brick oven. Steam rose from their shiny tops. There were cookies too; much different from the fortune cookies back home, but the smells brought back good memories.

"This market is huge," she thought, dodging all kinds of clothes being shoved along on hanging racks and being put into delivery trucks. *I guess this stuff is being distributed all across the city.*

Finally coming out of the market, Char-Lee looked at the map again and turned west into the heart of the city toward her aunt's house. After several blocks she saw a street sign for the street their shop should be on. It was a wide street with many other shops. But after a few steps she saw the name, 'Lieu Chan Market' on an awning and stepped inside.

After the sunny day outside, the shop was dim and cool, stuffed to the brim with everything from fruits and vegetables to canned goods, tools, clothes and in the rear a cold case filled with meat and chicken.

"Hello, Aunty. I just had my interview and Mr. Xiang hired me. I start work tomorrow."

Charlie's Tale

"Welcome, Char-Lee. That is very good news. Come, and let me show you around our store."

Uncle was busy in the back with a customer but waved hello. After the little tour, Char-Lee spent the rest of the day helping, bringing stock up from the basement and setting things on shelves.

"You have been a great help today, Char-Lee, but it is late now. Why don't you leave and go by way of Grandmother's laundry. You can accompany her home," Aunty suggested.

She drew another simple map for Char-Lee and off she went, peering into shops and nodding hello to the shopkeepers. Grandmother was surprised to see Char-Lee. She was folding laundry and asked her to sit for a few minutes while she finished up. Ah-Choo was right about this place too. It was hot and steamy and smelled of soap and dirty laundry.

Setting off for home, Char-Lee asked Grandmother how long she had worked there and what she did before the laundry.

"Work here many years now, Char-Lee. Laundry my own business. I born in same house we live now in 1937. Several years before I born, Japan invade north China and when I born, Japan marching south to conquer all China."

"At that time, China have two political parties fighting for control, the Nationalist Party and the Communist Party. So busy fighting each other, no problem for Japanese to control country."

Charlie's Tale

"We live through Japanese reign of terror and World War II. People starving. Working for Japan war industries. People coming from countryside to big cities to work. Not working on farms so very little food."

"Other people coming into country, too, running away from war in West. My father, he work with Jewish people, Polish people lots of other people coming into China. They work right along with all of us until end of war. By then I eight years old, but much older in head from listening and watching all the people."

"After war, went to school. Can read and write, Char-Lee. Everybody busy rebuilding country. After school I meet husband in government office where we both work. When he die, I buy laundry."

"When did the communists take over, Grandmother?"
"After war Japan gone, 1945-1946, China need new government. Mao Tsi Tung proclaim People's Republic of China."

"What about religion. Did your parents go to a temple to worship?"

"No, no, while I young, worship Buddha and old gods in home. Sometime go to Temple before government say, 'no more gods', only communism, everyone must belong to Communist Party."

"What about now, Grandmother? Have you gone back to worshiping the old gods?"

Charlie's Tale

"No, child. Don't think about gods. Think about being good person and do no evil to anyone."

"Now tell me about place where you come from. I never been away from Shanghai."

"We lived in a small village in Hubei Province near the big city Yichang. Have you ever heard of the great Three Gorges Dam, Grandmother? This is near Yichang City. Hubei is an ancient Chu culture. There are many temples and palaces, especially on the Taoist sacred Wudang Mountain. But our village is a simple place, maybe fifty houses, a market square, a bath house and an old Buddha temple. My family prayed to Buddha and the old gods."

"Yes, that is the way of village people, child. Ah, here we are. Good to be home. Feet tired," she signed.

* * *

They had arrived back at the house and Char-Lee set about helping Old Grandmother prepare dinner for the family. As they chopped vegetables and made noodles, she asked her again to tell about the Monkey God.

"Other great god beside Jade Emperor is Monkey. Monkey loved to disobey the rules and caused much trouble in heaven and earth until Jade Emperor gave him a grand title. You know Char-lee that Jade Emperor is a master of DAO principle? 'To do nothing is best way to rule'. I will tell you more of Monkey another day; now I hear my daughter coming home."

Charlie's Tale

The next morning Char-Lee arrived a little early at the factory and was shown to her place at a sewing machine. She introduced herself to the women on either side of her. The older one to the right was named Su-Jen and the young girl to the left was named Mai Li.

As Char-Lee sat down, a woman from the end of the line of machines came over and introduced herself as Zu-Chee. "I am leader of this line," she explained. "Each line has leader who sits at end of row. I will show you what to do, bring you work for the day and pick up finished pieces. Today, you will sew back and side seams of all shirts in this basket. If you finish before end of day or need thread or needle, raise hand and I will bring. Welcome to work here."

"Thank you Zu-Chee. I will do my best for you, Char-Lee replied."

With that, she picked up a set of pieces, watched how the women on either side of her worked and began the new job. *What a difference from pounding nails into lumber! Though I had to be careful not to run the needle through my fingers, at least I wouldn't be hitting them with a hammer!*

When it was time for lunch, a bell rang. All work stopped. Everyone brought out the food they had brought from home and sat around eating and chatting with one another. The machines were smack up against each other and there was hardly any room between the lines, so they were all nearly on top of each other.

Charlie's Tale

The ladies nearby asked a million questions, wanting to know all about Char-Lee. The older lady, Su-Jen was pleased to say she knew Char-Lee's Auntie. Mai Li had just finished school and was also new at the factory. Then, before she knew it the bell rang and it was back to work.

That evening, the bell rang again for the end of the day and everyone put away their work and began to file down the stairs. Char-Lee noticed that Mr. Xiang unlocked the door and held it open as everyone left. There was no inside bar on the door to open if there was an emergency. The door was kept locked until Mr. Xiang opened it and held it open.

* * *

Old Grandmother approached Char-Lee soon after the first week at work. "Char-Lee, I would like to go to Longhua temple. There is no work tomorrow. You will come with me?"

"How will we get there, Old Grandmother? You cannot walk far."

"Neighbor will take in rickshaw, but not so far. Have not been for long time and wish to see again before I die."

"You are not planning to die soon, are you?"

"No child, but one cannot defy fate."

The next morning, after some cold rice and hot tea, they went next door and met Mr. Lin, a small, muscular man with very creased, very tan, weathered skin. He was dressed in long, side-slit trousers and a big straw hat. He sat the two of them in his rickshaw and got onto a bike attached to the front.

It was an interesting sensation being pulled along the streets. I felt like a rich person or maybe a king with his own personal chauffer. The cart kind of bumped along, mixing with cars, mopeds and bicycles. The sun was shining down and I enjoyed it immensely. After about fifteen minutes, I spotted a beautiful, old temple with a seven story pagoda at the front.

Char-Lee helped Old Grandmother down and thanked Mr. Lin who said he would pick them up in an hour. Then they entered the beautiful temple grounds filled with wonderfully smelling peach blossoms.

Longhua Temple was founded in 247 A.D. as they were informed by a bronze plaque on a stand in the garden. The plaque went on to tell that the temple area had once been a prison and execution ground for the communist government. Longhua was the largest temple in the city. Its seven story brick and wood pagoda was an octagonal structure with each of the seven sections topped with upturned, flying eaves of grey tiles from which tiny bells were suspended.

There were four main halls, but the most impressive, Char-Lee thought, was the Grand Hall with its gilded statue of Buddha flanked on each side by eighteen disciples, all under a beautifully carved dome.

As they wandered through, looking at all the golden statues of Buddhist saints, the old lady explained they were men thought to have achieved enlightenment.

Charlie's Tale

"Will you tell me about Buddha, Old Grandmother?"

"At first, Char-Lee, Buddha was not a god. He was a great man. Dauist make him into a god later."

"Buddha teach people how to live in right way. He say there are five things to observe;

- Avoid killing or harming any living being.
- Avoid taking that which has not been given.
- Avoid committing sexual misconduct.
- Avoid using false words.
- Avoid taking alcohol and other intoxicants.

Also, but not so important to everyday person, just monks: must eat moderately, avoid dancing, singing, music and bodily adornments, and abstain from sleeping in luxurious beds."

"There are also four noble truths Buddha teach:

First, all worldly things are unsatisfactory. Existence is fleeting and unfulfilling, subject to birth, decay, disease and death.

Second, the cause of everything being unsatisfactory is the craving for pleasure of the senses, which can never be satisfied, and the aversion to pain.

Third, to be free of this unsatisfactory existence one must extinguish this craving so that no passion and desire remain. Fourth, the end of dissatisfaction is by way of the Eightfold Path to Enlightenment."

"What is the Eightfold Path, Old Grandmother?"

"A very hard path to follow, child, take years of study and concentration. The Eightfold Path is:

- Perfect Understanding,
- Perfect Thought,
- Perfect Speech,
- Perfect Action,
- Perfect Livelihood,
- Perfect Effort,
- Perfect Mindfulness, and
- Perfect Concentration."

"You see how difficult this can be? Someone who can achieve this is truly a saint."

"But, Old Grandmother, if Buddha is not a god, why do you pray to him?"

"Why, child, I pray for enlightenment, for understanding and the courage to live by Buddha's way."

"Thank you, I think now I understand. Buddha's ideas are very much like the religious laws of Judaism, Christianity and Islam that I was taught in school. Isn't it interesting that such different people living so far from each other believe in the same basic ideas?"

"I don't know about other peoples and their religions. It is hard enough to live by one's own truths Char-Lee."

* * *

Char-Lee had been in Shanghai for about a month, helping around the house and garden and occasionally in the shop and

Charlie's Tale

working in the factory. She was getting to know her way around the big city and went to several museums with her young cousin, Jan-Ping, but as yet she had no friends to hang out with. Then during lunch one day at work, Mai Li, the young worker next to Char-Lee asked if she would like to join her and some friends to go out to dinner and music over the week-end. Char-Lee was delighted about meeting and getting to know more young people.

She met Mai-Li outside the factory and they took a jitney bus to a place called, Goodfellas. The place was jammed to the walls with young people dancing to DJ music.

"Boy is this loud," Char-Lee shouted over the noise.

Mai-Li looked around and spotted her friends. *I don't know how she found them in the glittering, dim light. She took my hand and we wound our way through the dancers to a tiny, high table surrounded by six high stools with at least ten people sitting on them and more standing.*

As Mai-Li introduced me, one young man bellowed to a waitress for more beer all around.

Now the noise and the music weren't exactly my kind of thing. But, I sure blessed the beer delivered to the table by a fearless waitress carrying a tray full of mugs above the heads of the dancers. Everyone welcomed me, especially the boys who raised a rousing cheer to the new girl in town.

The people at the table kept changing depending on who was dancing and who was drinking and after a couple of beers I loosened up enough to join Mai-Li and a some guys on the dance floor. Everybody danced

Charlie's Tale

separately the way the kids at home did. No old fashioned cheek to cheek for them.

I couldn't tell you what name belonged to whom. But they were a great group of friendly, young Chinese. Before we finally called it a night, several of us agreed to meet the next day at a tea house and for a walk along the promenade by the river.

It had all been noisy, smoky, and full of laughter and lots of fun. I realized it had been like forever since I had had such a good time.

The next day, Char-Lee made her way to the tea house, immediately spotting Mai Li and her friends. They waved her over and as she sat down a waitress came for her order.

"A pot of tea," she ordered.

It was much easier to talk and listen in the busy but much quieter atmosphere of the café than it had been at Goodfellas, even though there were throngs of pedestrians walking by the outside tables.

"Char-Lee is from Hubei," Mai Li told the group. Then, she was flooded with a lot questions about the area, since most had never been far from Shanghai. She explained about her background and told them about the beauty of the Hubei Provence and its ancient culture.

"You should see the beautiful temples on the hills. I hope someday you will be able to travel and see more of the countryside. But right now, Char-Lee was more interested in finding out about them and Shanghai than talking about herself."

Charlie's Tale

Several boys and girls were university students. One boy was studying astronomy and specializing in the giant mirrors needed in space exploration. Two girls were into bio technology and another boy was getting his master's in government.

Two others had finished the American equivalent of high school and were working in factories or shops, though one young man, Jim Lee, professed to have art as his main interest and invited everyone to his room in a shared flat the following weekend to see his art work.

They spent a couple of hours just sitting, drinking tea, talking and getting to know one another and then ambled over to the promenade to walk along the water's edge.

How nice to be with friends, just sitting and talking in the lovely sunshine. I thought. *I haven't done this for a long time either. Why not, Charlie? I don't know. You just get into a lazy rut doing the same old thing every day and not thinking about your friends*, I said to myself.

When Char-Lee got home, the family, especially Jan Ping, wanted to know about everyone she had met.

"How many boys and girls were at the bar last night, Char-Lee? Did everybody dance? Did you dance, too?

"Jan Ping, there were so many people there I couldn't count them. The place was jammed and everybody was dancing. Me too."

Charlie's Tale

"What about at the café today," Auntie asked. "Were they a nice group of people?"

"Very nice, Auntie. Some were in college and some were working. We discussed Shanghai and Hubei, where we would like to visit and where we hoped to be in the future.

Everyone wanted especially to visit America, Britain and Germany. I enjoyed myself very much."

The family continued talking until it was time to go to bed.

Back at work, during lunch break, Mai-Li also wanted to know how Char-Lee had enjoyed herself and they discussed each of her friends and their hopes for the future."

* * *

At the end of the work week, Char-Lee found herself helping Old Grandmother and Jan Ping chop vegetables, fish and meat for dinner. Jan Ping was chatting away, but Char-Lee used a quiet moment to ask, "Old Grandmother, it is another day today. Will you tell us about the Monkey God?"

"Oh, children, Monkey is the trickster god with title of Great Sage Equal of Heaven. From the beginning of time, a certain rock on the Mountain of Fruit and Flowers had been soaking up the goodness of nature and energy. One day this pregnant rock released a stone egg, and from it hatched a Stone Ape, who solemnly bowed to the Four Corners of the Earth and then jumped off to have fun."

"Monkey high spirited, and full of mischief. He has a wonderful time being King of Apes. But he fear Death."

Charlie's Tale

"To find immortality, Monkey became disciple of Dauist sage Father Subodhi, where he learn cloud-flying and the secret of the seventy-two transformations."

"Returning home, Monkey discover his subjects under siege by a fearsome monster. He need a great weapon to defeat this monster. So, he steal great Magic Wishing Staff from Dragon King. This staff a huge rod of iron Heaven once use to flatten bed of Milky Way. Monkey use it to bludgeon many demons once he have it."

"But other gods complain to Jade Emperor of Monkey's mischief and thievery, so Jade Emperor invite Monkey to Heaven and give him job. This successful for one entire day. Then Monkey discover his job lower even than horse manure."

"Insulted, Monkey run amok and threaten Jade Emperor. The Ruler of the Universe consult with advisors and bestowed new title on Monkey: Great Sage, Equal of Heaven. Monkey happy but by his nature, still naughty. He just could not help it."

"Jade Emperor finally lose cool and send army to kill Monkey. But Monkey immortal. So, he beat army. Then Jade Emperor call on Buddha. Buddha make bet with Monkey.

"If you so clever, jump off palm of my hand. If you can do that, I'll take Emperor in as lodger and give Heaven to you. But if you can't, I will expect apology and penance."

Charlie's Tale

"Monkey think, 'this will be easy,' because he could travel several thousand miles in a single leap. Buddha held out his hand and Monkey jump and land in desolate plain with five great columns reaching to the sky. To show his disrespect, he piss all over nearest pillars, then jump back."

"Is the Emperor packing his bags yet?" asked Monkey.

"I don't know what you are grinning at, Buddha reply, you have been on my palm entire time. Sure enough when Monkey look, he astonished to see five pillars were the five great fingers of Buddha's hand and then he smelled his piss and was afraid. Next thing he knew, he lying on the ground with a mountain on top of him where he stay for five hundred years."

"Wow, Old Grandmother that was great. You are a great story teller."

Jan Ping was frowning. "You never told me this story before. I hope you will tell us more about the old gods, Old Grandmother. We don't hear these stories in school and I don't think my friends ever heard them."

"Another day, child, another day. Now it is time for my nap." As Old Grandmother went to lie down, Char-Lee asked Jan Ping what religion she practiced.

"My parents and I are Christians, Char-Lee. When Mao began allowing people to worship if they wished, my father remembered the British churches he visited in London when he worked for the government. My parents went to speak to

Charlie's Tale

one of the ministers of a church here and decided to join the congregation. They don't go to church every Sunday, but they like the idea that Jesus was a man as well as God. Also, Christianity seemed to have many of the same laws one must live by to be a good Buddhist. They are pleased with the church they chose. When I get older, I will choose for myself," she replied.

* * *

Sunday, Char-Lee headed over to Jim Lee's apartment to see his art work and brought Jan Ping along with her. By this time, she was calling Jan Ping, JP. JP was so excited to be going out with an older group she didn't stop talking for a minute until they got to Jim's. Then she didn't open her mouth the entire time they were there.

It was the usual group of friends plus Jim's roommate. They were spread out all over the two room apartment, lying over the couch and a couple of chairs or sitting on the floor. Jim offered tea and coffee, sweet biscuits and nuts.

JP and Char-Lee sat on the floor near Mai-Li. "I'm so pleased to meet you Jan Ping, Mai Li bowed. Char-Lee has told us all about you."

JP bowed too and smiled back. Blushing furiously, she turned and gave Char-Lee an evil look.

I looked about the room to take in Jim's paintings and sculpture. Of course, I'm no artist and I can't say I paid much attention, but the wife

Charlie's Tale

and I had taken the kids to several art shows in both the modern art and classic museums. "I guess something sank in," I thought.

I would call Jim's work abstract, pleasing shapes and forms. There was nothing I would call grotesque. The colors in the paintings were bold, not wishy-washy and it looked like he could really draw, not just splash paint on a canvas.

The sculptures were interesting because I was less familiar with abstract work in three dimensions.

Char-Lee walked over to Jim to tell him how much she liked his work.

"Jim, I don't know very much about art. But I like your work. Did you go to art school? Where did you learn so much?"

"No school, Char-Lee. My parents have no money for such extra things. But I have an uncle who once went to school for classic Chinese painting and he taught me many things. I did not like the strict forms of the classic Chinese painters. I wanted to paint with more freedom. So I went to galleries and museums and looked at Western art in books and on my computer."

"Shapes interest me, but also the way artists like Monet and even Ruben use light is a thing of beauty. Look at this painting over here." He pointed to a bright, mainly red and blue painting. "If you watch for a few minutes, you will see how the light moves across the painting and changes the colors, and even the shapes. This is what I am aiming at right now. I don't yet know how I will move on from this point."

Charlie's Tale

"Jim, that's wonderful. I'm going to watch this painting all afternoon to see it changing. Have you talked to any galleries about showing your work?"

"Yes, Char-Lee. But I am not ready as yet. There are several more paintings and at least one more sculpture I want to do first. I want to somehow get more shadows and light changes into the sculptures and I'm not sure how that will work out."

"In fact, Char Lee, you are very pretty and have a different physical appearance than the people of Shanghai. Perhaps you would sit as a model for me?"

"How very kind of you, Jim. The people from my village are all tall like me. I think it would be fun to see what you would make of me."

Char-Lee smiled, moving off as another friend asked Jim a question. "Good luck, Jim. Please let us know when you have your show."

As she was walking around the perimeter of the room so as not to stumble over someone, she heard a loud, "Hello." Looking around two people in deep conversation near her, Char-Lee discovered a large cage with two parrots standing on their perches.

"Hello there. Did you say hello to me?"

"Hello Spirit," one of them squawked. "Glad to have you here. Got a call from our balloon friends out yonder about you coming."

Charlie's Tale

"You mean you can talk with the other species so far away?" Char-Lee asked.

"Well, not directly, of course. But the grape vine works very well. Say, while you're visiting, would you do us a favor? Would you tell Jim we don't like the new food he is buying for us? We like the old seeds better."

Char-Lee laughed and smoothed their feathers through the cage bars. "Sure, boys. I'll be happy to help. See you later."

"Goodbye" they both squawked.

Char-Lee moved away from the bird cage and looked around to see if anyone had noticed she was talking to birds. But everyone was so busy talking to each other no one seemed to have noticed.

Chuckling to herself, Char-Lee picked up a dish of biscuits and moved toward Jim. *If I were myself instead of a girl,* I thought, *I would be bringing him a beer.*

"Have some of your own biscuits Jim, before your friends eat them all. I was just talking to your birds."

Jim smiled and took a biscuit. "Those two birds have learned a lot of new words since we brought them home."

"Yes, but I noticed they don't seem to like their food. We had the same kind of birds at home in Hubei and they wouldn't touch that kind of food. Perhaps you should think of making a change."

Charlie's Tale

"You think so, Char-Lee? They don't seem to be eating as usual. I'll try going back to the food I used to give them. Thanks."

Moving on, she bumped into Jim's roommate, Ali. Wearing a burnoose, he was very obviously from a Middle Eastern country.

"It's very nice of you to have us over, Ali. I am Char-Lee. I come from Hubei Province, but now I live with my aunt and uncle here in Shanghai and work at the shirt factory with Mai Li. Where do you come from?"

"Very nice to meet you Char-Lee. My family home is in Qatar and I am here to learn new bio-engineering techniques being researched in China. A group of us have been here about a year now."

"I'm assuming your religion is Islam. If so, you must find it hard to worship here. Are there mosques where you can go to pray and study or other Muslims who live here that your group can meet with? "

"There are a few, and we meet regularly at their mosque," he replied. I worship on a regular basis and, of course, pray five times a day as required by our faith. That I can do anywhere I happen to be."

"I know very little about Islam, Ali. Perhaps this is not the time or place, but I would like to know more. I have many questions because I do not understand your religion.

Charlie's Tale

Everything I have read talks about how Islam honors God and yet believes in killing those of other religions."

"Oh no, Char-Li. Like many people you misunderstand our faith. My father is an Imam, a leader of the faith, and so perhaps I am able to explain a little better than some.

First of all, Muslims share a belief in the six articles of faith which are the main doctrines of Islam.

Islam preaches that there is only one Supreme, Eternal, Infinite and Unparalleled entity, Allah (God). He is the creator of all the universe.

We believe in angels who are comprised of light and have different purposes to help Allah.

Muslims believe in all four books of scriptures; the Torah of Moses, the Psalms of David, the Gospel of Jesus and the Quran of Mohammad. But, we believe the Quran is the only book that has never been distorted through the ages.

Muslims also believe in the prophets, the messengers from Adam to Mohammad. We treat them all equally.

And we have faith that after the end of the world, every human will be resurrected from the grave, will be held accountable for what they have done in their lives and justice will be done to every soul. The innocent will stay in Heaven, but the corrupted will go to hell.

One of the main aspects of Islam is our belief in the divine creed of predestination; that God is not limited, even as to time; that everything that has happened, is happening, or will

Charlie's Tale

happen is evident to Him. Living beings have been given a free choice to do whatever we want to do. God knows what choice we will make but does not restrict us from making our own choices."

"Ali, those six basic ideas sound so much like the other great religions of the world. But, tell me, the newspapers talk about Sunnis and Shiites fighting all the time. What is that all about? And what about all these fanatics and terrorists who say their religion demands the killing of all infidels."

"First, Char-Lee, our people are also descended from Father Abraham. But, much later, the word of God was also revealed to Muhammad during a retreat in 610 A.D. He began preaching the word and gathering a following. The year 622 marks the founding of Islam as a religion."

"By Muhammad's death in 632, Islam had spread around the known world. Abu Bakr, a close companion of the Prophet, called a Caliph, became his successor. Abu Bakr's followers became the orthodox branch of Islam, the Sunnis."

"Some Muslims disagreed with having Abu Bakr as the successor, arguing for a succession based on bloodlines. They thought the succession should have gone to Ali, the fourth caliph, who was a blood relative of Muhammad. Followers of Ali would form Shiite Islam.

"Both sects believe in the same basic laws, but the application varies. Sunnis accept the first four Caliphs including Ali, but they don't grant the kind of divinely inspired status to their

Charlie's Tale

clerics that Shiites do their Imams. Shiites believe Imams are direct descendants of the Prophet."

"The majority of Muslims in the world follow the Shiite branch and are the majority in Iran, Iraq, Bahrain and Azerbaijan. Sunnis are the majority in Saudi Arabia, Egypt, Yemen, Pakistan, Indonesia, Turkey, Algeria, Morocco and Tunisia."

"I don't know why we have to fight each other. I guess it's all a matter of wanting power. The leaders want power more than they want what is good for their people."

"Secondly, Char-Lee, I believe that a great many people who join together in these terrorist groups are the disaffected poor who are looking for a way to overcome the social factors in their countries. In the armies they are fed, educated and have work to keep them busy. If the people were able to make a comfortable living, and understood more about the other people of the world through education and communication, they would not be able to be led so easily into evil. This is especially true of the younger generation."

"So, you too, believe that fighting between religions is often caused by religious and government leaders who are after power."

"Unfortunately, yes, I think you are right, Char Lee."

"You seem to be a very enlightened man Ali. I wish you well and hope that we can continue our discussion at some future

Charlie's Tale

time. Now, I think I had better collect my cousin, Jan Ping, and start for home before the family starts to worry about us."

"I would be most pleased to talk with you again, Char-Lee. Perhaps we can have a date for dinner one evening."

Having done her good deed for Jim's birds and had a very interesting discussion with Ali, albeit chuckling over the invitation to a date, JP and Char-Lee took their leave.

On the way home, JP talked a mile-a-minute about the people she had met and how she liked Jim's art work. "I'm going to buy some books and learn how to draw she informed Char-Lee. Will you come to the art galleries with me?"

"Sure JP. I'd love to."

During the week, JP made up a list of art galleries they could visit. She showed it to Char-Lee one evening after dinner and they narrowed their tour down to several in the same area. That way, Char-Lee suggested, they wouldn't be wasting time running all over the city. Fortunately, there were several galleries near the museums.

They started at the Shanghai Art Museum. Even though they were mainly interested in viewing modern art because of Jim's work, they decided to go along with a tour which was just starting and would encompass both classic Chinese work and the museum's current modern show. Of course, the classic work was beautiful; ancient bronzes, landscapes with their expressionist mountains and rivers all painted in fine, careful

Charlie's Tale

lines. Their tour guide, explained how rigidly correct the artists had to be to hold to the classic forms.

As they moved forward through the museum, they also moved forward in time and were able to see how Chinese art had changed over the centuries. Finally arriving at the current modern show, they realized the artists had become much freer in their work as the government had become more lenient.

They weren't holding to the strict lines and patterns demanded by the classics and the difference between the works of the modern artists and the ancient artists was extraordinary. According to the tour guide, today's artists were not letting themselves be limited by the past, but were often incorporating some of the ideals of the past in new ways.

The guide pointed out several particular artists and discussed their work, but JP and Char-Lee decided they especially liked the work of Feng Zhengjie which was very Pop Art, again according to the tour guide.

After the museum, they went to a district called the Bund. Here three artists had begun a modern art revolution. King Yi, Zhong Jiajun and Li Shan were professors and teachers who started a place for modern artists to work at this location in the 1980s. Now the Bund was a very popular place to work or visit.

They strolled through galleries and studios with a lot of other visitors and then sat at a tea café to rest and discuss art.

Charlie's Tale

"Char-Lee, our guide at the museum told me that they have art classes I could join and the cost is very little. I'm going to talk to Mom and Dad about taking a class to see what I can do."

"That's wonderful, JP. I know you'll enjoy it, but don't be too impatient. It takes time to learn anything and even more time to become good at what you are trying to do. Just look at Jim's work. His newer paintings are much better than his first ones, don't you think?"

"You're right. If I like the class and can learn some basics techniques, I'll keep working at it. I'm so glad you came with me today, Char-Lee. It was really fun."

"I had a great time too, JP"

* * *

The following week there was a worker's holiday. Everything was closed. Families went to the parks, the zoo, walked along the promenade or sailed on the river. People took picnic lunches and sat under trees. Some of the older people danced in the parks or played games of all sorts. Grandmother decided she would like to walk in the park and asked Char-Lee to accompany her. Char-Lee was very pleased since she had not had much chance to speak with Grandmother.

They walked quietly along the park paths watching the old men at their chess and stopped to watch the dancers. "Char-Lee, come dance with me," she smiled. "It has been a long time since I had some exercise."

Charlie's Tale

They were playing a recording of some old time, slow, Western songs, so Char-Lee took Grandmother's hand and they started dancing along with the others.

Grandmother led and that was different. The music and the dancing brought back memories of Julie and me at our high school prom. I missed her terribly.

The song ended and the two walked on for a while. Stopping again, they joined a group of people watching a ping pong game. The players were very serious and the people cheered for their favorite.

"Grandmother," Char-Lee said, "I do not see you praying to Buddha like Great Grandmother. Why is that? Do you not believe?"

"Believe ideas of Buddha, Confucius, and Christianity good. Not know much about other religions. But do not think many religious people live by their god's rules. I hear of Christian Crusades. I hear of Jahadists in Africa and Hitler holocaust in World War II."

"As I told you before, when I born 1937, China have two political parties fighting for control. One is Nationalist Party with Chiang Kai-shek, leader. Other is Communist Party with Zedong leader. Japan push both parties out to far western China into exile. Then kill thousands as they conquer the land."

"After Second World War happen and Japan defeated, China in very bad shape, people starving. Two parties start fighting again. Finally, Mao push Nationalist Party out of mainland to Taiwan. Then Communist Party rule China."

"When leader, Zedong die, Mao proclaim People's Republic of China. Everyone is to work for the government. Government own everything, give people what they need. Religion forbidden. Many ancient temples looted, torn down, others made into government buildings. Everyone put to work."

"Ruling party say religion no good, opiate of the people. Parents never show me how to pray, so I do this my way."

"So you don't believe in the ancient gods, Buddha or any other religion, Grandmother?"

"Very religious men study Buddha all time. To achieve enlightenment they must study hard and meditate while they contemplate navel. Women have no time to contemplate naval. Must always work; give birth, care for children and men, cook, wash, clean and work at job for money so men have time to contemplate navel."

"As for Great God, man lives always conscious of time because he know his time limited. Great God has no time. Just Is. I am too small to understand Great God, but try to live according to good ideas of Buddha."

"You are very wise, Grandmother."

Oh, boy, this is a lot to chew on. Again, people following leaders, but this time government leaders who do not want the people influenced by religious leaders. I guess this happens a lot too. Then there were the government and religious leaders who decided they wanted to be both

Charlie's Tale

religious and government leaders, like some of the popes and kings. A lot to think about!

* * *

Mai-Li smiled as they settled themselves at their sewing machines. "You are happy here in Shanghai, Char-Lee?"

"Yes, Mai Li, especially since I met you and your friends. Thank you for including me."

Everyone worked along for a while and then, Char-Lee noticed the mild smell of smoke. Others seemed to notice at the same time, especially the ironers at the back of the room. The leader of that line was checking all the machines and electric plugs. But everything seemed to be alright. So they all turned back to their work.

But, within a few minutes, the smell had increased and the people in the back of the room were coughing and wiping their eyes. Smoke began to drift gently across the ceiling. Many of the machines stopped as workers became concerned. Char-Lee was able to hear sirens in the distance. As the sirens grew louder the smoke became heavier.

I may not have learned a lot in school, but the visit by a local fireman stuck in my head. He showed us pictures of various fires and the firemen fighting them. He explained the need for important safety codes to be put into effect while buildings were being constructed and that these codes had to be kept active for the sake of the workers and the people living and working in them in the future.

Charlie's Tale

Several of the photos and information he showed came from the shirt factory fire in New York. I'll never forget those pictures of people jumping from windows and firemen and workers being carried out.

Mr. Xiang's door was closed and Char-Lee didn't think he could smell the smoke. But she remembered the locked entrance/exit door.

"Someone should tell Mr. Xiang about the smoke," Char-Lee said aloud. But no one seemed to want to approach the boss. The sirens were very loud by now and seemed to be right outside the building. Char-Lee didn't see any flames, but, people were coughing badly from the smoke. Thankfully, there was no panic, yet.

Remembering the horrendous loss of life in the New York factory fire, Char-Lee got up, made her way to Mr. Xiang's office and opened the door.

"Mr. Xiang, excuse me for interrupting you, but have you not noticed the smoke in the factory. It is getting worse. Those in the back cannot see to work and fire equipment is outside."

Mr. Xiang looked up, shot out of his chair and ran into the big room. When she turned to follow, Char-Lee saw the back wall was cracking. It sounded like rifle shots. Flames were coming through the cracks. The workers in the back were beginning to move toward the stairs. In a minute, there would be panic.

"Mr. Xiang," Char-Lee called. "You have to open the front door." She grabbed the key from its hook by the door and handed it to Mr. Xiang who was standing paralyzed with fear. She pushed him toward the stair. As he hurried down to open the door, she shouted to everyone to move slowly, there was plenty of time to get out. But, they were rushing forward and pushing those in front of them. How could she stop the panic? What would get their attention?

"Money, Money" she shouted.

That caught everyone's attention and she shouted again to calm down and follow their line leaders, that the front door was open and they would be safe if they dept calm.
"Just move forward line by line down the stairs and you will be all right."

She called to the leaders to control their lines and everyone began moving in an orderly way, quickly toward the stairs, down and outside. Once they reached the street, they could see that the building next door was on fire. The two buildings were so close together that the fire had spread to Mr. Xiang's building.

There were two fire trucks on the street. The firemen seemed to be doing all they could to keep the fire from spreading.

This could get out of control and take the whole block, Char-Lee thought. *They need more men and trucks.* Within a couple of minutes, more help did arrive.

It took all morning to quench the fire which destroyed the top two floors of the building where it started. But the firemen managed to save the other buildings on the street. Mr. Xiang

Charlie's Tale

had been talking with the owner of the factory that was on fire. But he finally turned and told everyone to go home. Gradually, all the watchers wandered slowly off the street while the firemen cleaned up.

A story about the fire was in the evening newspapers and the Lieu family was all excited and had Char-Lee explaining what it was like and retelling the story all evening.

* * *

There was no work the next day so Char-Lee went to the shop to help Auntie and Uncle. Arranging the fruit and vegetables with Auntie, she had a chance to talk with her.

"Fire is a very scary thing, Auntie," she said as they carefully arranged tomatoes in a bin. I was praying the whole time that no one would get hurt."

"Who do you pray to, Char-Lee?"

We had a Buddha shrine in our home, Auntie Woo, but we went to the Christian church.

"And you? JP tells me you and Uncle are Christian. What drew you to Christianity?"

"Uncle and I know Buddha and old gods from Old Grandmother, but learn about western religions from contact with people in other countries while we work at computer company. Western business people come to China. Uncle visit England on business.

Charlie's Tale

"Uncle make good friend in London. Visit with family. Learn about Christianity. Visit churches with new friends. Now we Protestant. Believe in God and son Jesus. Same as Buddha thinking but can be forgiven for sins and saved because of Jesus dying for our sins."

"Why did you choose to become a Protestant, Auntie, why not some other denomination?"

"Catholic too orthodox must confess all time, pray to Virgin and Saints. Protestant more for today people, easier to live with. Like sermons, especially like what Jesus say in 'The Beatitudes':

- Blessed are the poor in spirit, for theirs is the kingdom of heaven.
- Blessed are those who mourn, for they will be comforted.
- Blessed are the meek, for they will inherit the earth.
- Blessed are those who hunger and thirst for righteousness, for they will be filled.
- Blessed are the merciful, for they will receive mercy.
- Blessed are the pure in heart, for they will see God.
- Blessed are the peacemakers, for they will be called children of God.
- Blessed are those who are persecuted for righteousness sake, for theirs is the kingdom of heaven.

Charlie's Tale

- Blessed are you when people revile you and persecute you and utter all kinds of evil against you falsely on my account. Rejoice and be glad, for your reward is great in heaven, for in the same way they persecuted the prophets who were before you."

"It is much like Buddha and Confucius but more modern and very beautiful to think about. Other people in China choose Buddha, Tao, Islam, Catholic and Confucius."

"Uncle and I both born 1970, Char-Lee. Mother and Father strict communist. No religion. Grandmother very quiet about Buddha and old Gods. No Buddha shrine in house."

"Six years old in 1976 when student revolt start. On June 4, 1989, pro-democracy people gather in and around Tianamen Square to protest hardship and laws of administration."

"Deng and Elders call out Red Guard and State soldiers to attack people with guns and tanks. Hundreds killed. People in uproar, frightened."

"Deng and government send troops and Red Guard to two hundred more cities to stop pro-democracy. Many, many people killed."

"Afterward, government send students and young people away from cities, out to work in countryside to learn proletarian values, they say. Families pulled apart. Red Guard ravaging countryside to punish, kill anyone not strict communist."

Charlie's Tale

"Father killed. Mother come back to Shanghai to live with Old Grandmother. Grandfather dead too. I finish school and go to university where I meet Uncle. After while, Government allow people to quietly go back to old beliefs not so strict now about religion."

"Glad China changing. People can decide many things for selves now, work for selves now. Learning so much about rest of world. But leaders right, you know. We must listen and obey laws. China very large country, many, many people. Must be patient. Government must have firm control of country to bring change slowly while everyone in country educated."

So now I see how a China that survived years of war is being influenced by Western religions. Maybe their government is being influenced by Western ways too. But it's a big country with a huge population. I think change is going to take a long time.

* * *

The next day, there was some cleaning up to do at the factory before work could begin, but it wasn't too bad. Mr. Xiang had some men working to repair the back wall which had caved in at one section. The ironing line was shifted to the side walls to make room for the repair people to do their work.

Mr. Xiang came out of his office as we started work and called for attention.

Charlie's Tale

"I wish to thank Miss Char-Lee for calling my attention to the fire before anyone could get hurt. She is our hero." He handed Char-Lee a bouquet of flowers and everyone clapped. Char-Lee bowed, said thank you and sat back down, embarrassed to death. Later, at lunch break many people came over to thank her. She told them they were all heroes for not running in a panic that might have caused harm to some of them.

When Char-Lee got home that evening, Old Grandmother handed her a letter. It was not often anyone received mail and she was very anxious that it should not mean bad news. Char-Lee opened the letter and read it aloud. It was a notice from the education department of the government saying they wished Char-Lee to go back to her village and become a teacher.

Tears started rolling down Old Grandmothers old face. "You will be leaving us now, Char-Lee. Very sad but good opportunity for you."

And indeed, the family, especially JP, was very sad, but, Charlie understood this was his call back to heaven. Hubei was far from Shanghai and the family would not expect much contact from Char-Lee. They would not expect to ever see Char-Lee again.

PART 4

CHAPTER 11

Char-Lee packed up his things into the old pack, hugged everyone and walked down the street with Ah-Choo following along. As he turned the corner, he stopped and petted the dog.

"Good bye friend. I hope to see you again."

"Have a good trip Spirit. It was nice meeting you," Ah-Choo replied. "Don't forget to give a dog a bone once in a while."

"I won't forget, pal," Charlie laughed.

A couple of more steps and Charlie was off and flying away into the sparkling night of the universe. He was no longer afraid, feeling comfortable that he was being taken care of.

"I wonder why we didn't have a dog. Even a cat would have been okay. The kids used to beg for a dog when they were real little. I guess they got tired of asking. Julie always said, 'over my dead body'. 'Course I can't blame her. She had plenty to do and she would have probably ended up being the one to take care of any pet. Ah-Choo was a good dog. I'll miss him. I'll really miss everybody.

Then, before he could think much more about his friends, he came to the beautiful, bright light that was now Meg.
"Hi, beautiful. That purple color looks good on you."

Charlie's Tale

"And did you notice you're red now, Charlie? Welcome back"

"You're right, Meg. I hadn't noticed my new color. I guess this means I'm making some progress. Right?"

"Yes, you are, Charlie. Now, I can't wait to hear all about China. I've never been there and I'm very excited to find out about that country and what you learned."

"What an interesting place, Meg. I learned so much. The Lieu family was great; a Great Grandmother, a Grandmother, a middle aged couple and their daughter, Jan Ping. I really liked living with them. And, oh yes, I forgot Ah-Choo, their dog. Can't forget him. He was my guide."

"This time, even though it was the same year I died, I realized how different China was, such an ancient place. Their society is thousands of years older than America. I wish I had been able to visit more of the country. It's so big and has so many different kinds of people. But, there are few roads outside of the areas around the big cities and traveling is still very slow. Cell phones are spreading like hot cakes though and they're building roads and railroads as fast as they can. I can imagine how hard it was to govern that country in the old days without phones and barely any decent roads."

"What about today's government, Charlie?"

"The government is still pretty stiff with a lot of tuff rules. But, China is growing by leaps and bounds into a modern, busy country. It's still real different from the States though.

Charlie's Tale

The way the people think is so different. The freedom of each person is so much a part of America, but the Chinese are much more likely to think of themselves as a group instead of as individuals. I was told by one man that he would feel uncomfortable in a society where all the faces were different. How do you like that? I hope he gets to America one day."

"Oh, and Meg, the government hasn't done much of anything about things like work safety laws. But they are making a lot of headway in education and health issues."

"They have eased on some things and everyone wants to open his own business now. People work very hard and save every penny so they can set up a shop or small factory of their own. They're able to buy more cars and trucks too and the government encourages the population to buy because they are trying to get more industries started. That, of course, will mean more jobs for their huge population."

"Why do you think the government is easing up, Charlie?"

"I think they are trying to keep a better balance of things. A lot of people are leaving the countryside and coming to the cities. And while they need people to work in the factories, they also need enough farmers to feed all the people in the growing population. If the people have work and enough food, they'll be more content and it will be easier to govern."

"What about religion, Charlie? I know the old communist government forbade religious worship for a long time. What about now?"

Charlie's Tale

"The government has eased up on religious worship too, Meg, and the choices of the people are very interesting."

"I found that the ancient gods of the land and the home are still worshipped. But, with the government making things easier, Buddha and Confucius have come back strong. As far as I could tell, these ideas are more a way of living than of worship. Their beliefs are very like Judaism and Christianity."

"I also had a very interesting talk with a young man from the middle-east who was studying in China. From what he told me, Islam has similar ideals. They accept the Torah and the New Testament as well as the Quran."

"Now, with better communication and travel China is becoming more open and Christianity has been taken up by many younger people who were brought up during the time religion was banned and who don't know very much about the ancient gods."

"Wow, you have learned a lot, Charlie. So how did you like being a woman, she laughed?"

"It certainly gave me a different view of things, Meg. I think people were more open to me as a woman. I didn't like having a smaller body, but my understanding of people and the things around me were definitely increased. How I talked to people and treated them was more important to me than when I was a man."

"Well now, Charlie, you're in for something different again."

"Uh, oh! What now?"

Charlie's Tale

"Wait and see, Charlie. It's a surprise."

And, guess what, before I knew it, I was off again.

You're really getting this flying, Charlie, my boy. Just zipping along to wherever you want to go.

Charlie's Tale

Charlie's Tale

CHAPTER 12

"Hey, stop that!" I felt the first splashes of sunlight coming through the leaves of a tree, but that wasn't what woke me up. Maybe if I didn't open my eyes it would go away. PLOP!..PING!... Something was definitely attacking me from above.

I opened one eye, only to see a small red squirrel chattering at me from the branch of a tree while he cracked and ate some nuts.

"Hey, squirrel, stop that. Why are you dropping acorns on me? That hurts."

"Time to wake, Charlie. I'm just having my breakfast. It's a beautiful day."

I reared my neck and stretched my legs. That didn't feel right! My head felt so heavy. Had I gotten drunk last night?

I opened both eyes. I was lying in sweet smelling, dew wet grass with the early morning sun filtering down through the trees. As I pushed up from the ground and stood up, I knew something was very different. Looking down, I saw a pair of legs with hoofs. Trying to look between my legs brought a large pair of antlers banging down into the ground. So then, I swung a long neck back over my shoulder and saw a long, brown back and two more legs with hoofs, AND A TAIL?!

Charlie's Tale

"Okay, antlers. What am I, squirrel? A moose, an elk?"

"Of course not, Charlie, you're a deer. The biggest stag in these mountains."

"Oh, well then. That's just perfect. What am I supposed to learn as a deer?"

"Good morning," Charlie, something whispered with a sigh and a rustle.

Startled, I jerked my head up and looked around. I didn't see, hear or smell anything wrong.

Talk about hear and smell! Wow! What a collection. I thought I could smell everything in the forest and hear into the next county. But my eyes were different. I could see way around to the side but looking straight ahead was strange. I had to turn my head to see in front of me.

"Who's there?" I yelped. "Who said hello?"

"It's just me, Charlie" an oak tree sighed.

"Trees can talk?!"

"Oh, yes, Charlie. Even the flowers and ferns can speak and feel and even move about."

"I guess I should be used to strange things by now, Mr. Oak. Why, you must be at least fifty feet tall. What's it like up there?"

Charlie's Tale

"Actually almost eighty feet and it's nice and clear up here today. No clouds on the horizon. No tree men or hunters coming that I can see."

"Tree men?"

"Yes, the men who cut us down and the men who kill. It's my turn to be on watch and warn the forest today. No fires either, thank God."

"You believe in God?!"

"Of course. None of us would be here without God."

At that moment, several deer entered the clearing, clearly interested in who I was and what I was doing there.

A little fellow approached, tentatively nosing at me. When I lifted my head he jumped back and ran to his mother, cowering under her.

"Hello, everyone, I'm Charlie."

"Hello, Spirit," the little one's mother replied gently. "Welcome to the forest. How can we help you?"

"I'm just here to live with you for a while. I want to learn more about your lives here on earth."

"My name is Juniper, Spirit Charlie. The others are Jenny, Pine, Spruce and Max and my faun is Lolly. Come along and graze with us. We are going to the upper meadow today where water should be plentiful."

"Thank you Juniper and hello to the rest of you."

Charlie's Tale

The herd turned as one and moved slowly through the forest nibbling on leaves and sprigs of flowers.

"You have a nice group here," I said to Juniper.

"Yes, she replied. And Pine will soon have a new born. Unfortunately, we lost Big John last fall. The hunters got him."

"What happened?"

"The trees told us they were coming and Big John was urging us toward the deep canyons in the upper mountains, but as the hunters drew closer, he decided to lead them away. He ran to the top of a hill and showed himself and they chased after him, allowing the rest of us to escape. We don't know what happened, but we heard the guns and our hearts flew away. We never saw John again."

"You know, Charlie, we understand that all of us have to eat and some graze while others eat meat. But man grows plants and pens animals for his food. Why does he need to kill wild animals?"

"Long ago, man and animals used to move with the weather, with the growth in different seasons, to find food. Man killed to eat as the wolves do. Now, we are forced to follow man to find food because man is everywhere. The trees are chopped down. Meadows are burned. His buildings creep more and more into our world.

"There are fewer places to find food and water away from man. The birds go with the trees and the small animals flee."

Charlie's Tale

"You may not know this, Juniper, but man has made laws now, rules, that control hunting and also rules that control cutting down the trees. In most places they can only hunt once a year, in the fall and must not kill the little ones. There is also a limit to how many animals they can kill."

"We have some good people called Rangers whose job it is to protect the forest from humans who disobey the rules and also to protect the forest from fires. People don't want fire to kill the beasts and the forest."

"What about the humans who cut down the trees, Charlie. They destroy the forest too."

"Many places now have laws allowing only so much to be cut and they must be replaced with young trees. Unfortunately wood from trees is used for many good purposes by humans. But they are trying to use other materials and also to save and re-use the wood, so there will be less cutting."

"I can understand if there is a need. We eat the tree leaves and sometimes even the bark if we are hungry."
"Man has good feelings when he finds food and brings it home to his family. These are ancient feelings that are still in our blood, instincts like your instinct to hide from men because you know they will kill you.

"Part of man's new rules say that humans may not kill an animal for just one part to hang on their wall. They must make use of the entire animal as food or other useful things.

Charlie's Tale

"These rules are not everywhere in the world yet, but humans are changing. Though I know there are still plenty of people who don't obey the rules."

By now, we were in a lovely meadow, high in the mountains. "Surely the hunters don't come up here after you, Juniper?"

"Ah, but the fires do and then the water has no place to stay and runs away down the mountain. And sometimes even the mountains run away with the water, after a big fire. We live in fear, Charlie."

We continued to munch on the grass in the quiet of the beautiful day. Little Lolly played among the flowers and between the trees at the edge of the clearing. I eventually found myself close to some of the trees and looked up at a bright red cardinal calling to its mate.

"Hello Spirit, a whisper came from the tree. We knew you were coming. Welcome from all of us. I am known as Old Oak."

"Very nice to meet you, Old Oak. I suppose I shouldn't be surprised that the trees can speak. I've always heard them rustle and sing in the wind. You're a very old tree. I guess you've seen plenty in your time."

"Oh, yes, Charlie. There used to be trees as far as I could see. And many more trees where there are now deserts.

Continents have moved, weather has changed, comets have fallen and of course, there is Man."

Charlie's Tale

"How in the world can you know all of this, about continents and deserts and such?"

"Trees can see through time and through the universe, Charlie. I am aware of the two planets that you visited before you came back to earth. In fact, the butterflies who visit me are cousins of the butterflies on Blue's planet. Blue is also an old friend. Muffin's family were also friends when they lived on their original planet. It is a shame that planet exploded. It was very beautiful."

"I understand you can see what's going on around you because you're so tall. But how exactly do you know these other things?"

"Well, for one thing, we trees can communicate with one another. We speak across the world, but also our minds speak across time and space. That is how God made us so that we could be of use. This is God's design.

"Our job here is to shade, feed, house and act as watchers. But we also act as watchers for the entire planet and beyond. What happens in one place can affect any place and every place in God's universe."

"So even trees believe in God?"

"Of course, Charlie. We are all made by and are a part of God. We live and die by God's law as do all living things."

"Thank you, Old Oak for answering my questions."

The herd and I grazed and slept and moved on from glen to canyon to glen for a number of days or weeks. Time meant

Charlie's Tale

nothing. Everything was full of peace. I was at peace and one with them.

Smelling smoke one evening, I thought I had better check it out. The trees were quiet. They had no warning for us. But I asked Old Oak what he saw.

"Two of the caretakers have made a small fire nearby," he replied. "It is a proper man fire so I see no trouble."

"Okay, but I think I'll have a look-see anyway."

It took a while to approach quietly so they wouldn't see me. Standing in the shadows of a huge rock and behind some raspberry bushes, I saw two rangers sitting at a small camp fire having some dinner. It smelled like chicken and coffee. Yes, there was a pot of coffee on a grate over the fire. Boy that smelled good. I realized I hadn't had any coffee since I was with the Stillwell family.

The two men were dressed in khaki pants and plaid shirts and vests with their National Park badges stitched to them. Wide brimmed hats sat on the ground next to them and their equipment and camping gear were piled to the side.

Listening in, I heard them talking about the forest.

"Hunting season's coming on fast, Joe, said the larger of the two. Think we'll have some stud shooting up somebody from his own party this year?"

"Always some bozo who doesn't know what he's doing, Bob. Anyway, speaking of the season, we better get out our long

Charlie's Tale

johns and chop some more wood for the cabin to get ahead of winter."

"We might not get too much snow this winter, Joe; it's been a real dry summer. Good thing we had some luck this year with only that small fire at camp site number one. We got to her before she blew out of control."

"Right you are, Bob. We been real lucky this year."

The men finished their supper and crawled into their sleeping bags. Pretty soon their snoring joined the night sounds of the forest.

"Who, Spirit. Good evening to you." I shifted in surprise, but then saw the Great Horned Owl sitting in a pine tree.

"Good evening to you too, Mr. Owl," I replied. "You on watch tonight?"

"Yes, it's up to me in this section of the forest. You might want to keep your eyes open, Spirit. The wolves are hunting tonight."

"Thank you. I'll go tell the herd to set a bigger watch. With that, I backed out of the bushes and headed back to the herd.

* * *

One bright morning, not long after seeing the rangers, everything changed. The leaves were turning red and brown. The air was cold. The birds were calling sharply. Squirrels were chattering away and small animals were skittering one

Charlie's Tale

way and another. The herd picked up their heads, ears perked forward, listening. Juniper looked to the trees.

I could hear them too.

"Run, Run" they whispered. *"Hunters!"*

And the herd took off. Climbing higher and higher, into and out of deep canyons. Shots could be heard in the distance. We moved up and over the top of the mountain range and down into a deep forest where we could no longer hear the guns.

"What news?" Juniper asked a tall spruce.

"All is well for now," it answered. "But one of your kind is down along with several birds and rabbits. There should be no more today."

"Does this happen often," I asked Juniper.

"Often this time of year, but even sometimes at other times of the year. We have to always be cautious."

Two days later, we were back on the east side of the mountain around a large lake. We heard the trees rustling and knew people were in the woods, but there were no gun shots, so we were just snoozing in the afternoon sun.

All of a sudden shots rang out. I felt a hot explosion in my body and I was down. The others flew away around the lake and into the forest.

My head buzzed and my body felt cold and hurt like hell. Then three pairs of eyes were peering down at me.

Charlie's Tale

Oh...My...God! It's my brother Bud and my two kids. They were all excited and knelt down near my head. Then the kids really took a good look at me. My daughter, Jean starting crying and my son, Joe had tears in his eyes.

I looked deeply into their souls. Down into the deep pool of their hearts. *This is not right,* I tried to tell them. *You don't need to kill for food. Don't ever hunt for sport again. Take care of everything on God's great earth and say hello to your mother for me. I love you all.*

And then I was called away.

PART 5

CHAPTER 13

I passed through the cool dark skies and the brilliant stars with a feeling of peace and contentment, while the lights of the souls surrounded me with their warmth as I eased closer to the now deep, blue light that was Meg.

"Hi, Meg. It looks like I'm dead again," Charlie chuckled. "But at least I got to see my kids one last time. Thank you."

"You've done very well, Charlie. And just so you know, you were able to set your kids on the right path. They'll never go hunting again. Your son, Joe will become a veterinarian and your daughter, Jean, will become a biologist. Even your brother will give up hunting for sport."

"That's great. Thanks for telling me. I feel much better about having to leave them while they're so young."

"Now, Charlie, I'm anxious to know what you've learned through all of your trips."

"I think I have more questions than answers, Meg.

"First, I guess early man was pretty limited by his surroundings and his senses and fears. He was afraid of the dark, didn't understand about the stars and the things of the earth; nature, weather, the sun and moon. It was so hard to find food, not to mention birth and death. So I think man made up gods that meant something to him."

Charlie's Tale

"How do you mean, Charlie?"

"Well like he needed something to protect him from the unknown and hardship of everyday life; so he made up a god of thunder, a god to protect him from volcanoes, a water god and a sun or moon god, a god of the hunt and a god of the fire; a god to protect the birth of a child and a god to protect the dead. Personal gods, you know. There was no way those olden people could understand anything about the universe. I don't understand myself. Do you?"

I can see they must have felt so small compared to the land the sky. There was no way they would believe only one god could protect 'em.

"But, I think as time went on, man came to understand that there is only one Great God who created everything and is in charge.

Once upon a time, the Bible says, a man called Abraham came to believe there was only one God and people think of him as the father of Judaism, Christianity and Islam. His idea changed man and changed the world.

"You have been thinking, Charlie," Meg nodded. "But what about now. Have you figured out anything about good and evil? That was one of your big questions."

"I decided God found that man still needed to become more civilized and He chose the Jewish people and their prophet Moses to spread the word through The Ten Commandments.

Charlie's Tale

If man could only live by these Commandments, everything would be fine.

"What do you think of that idea, Meg?"

"I think you're on the right track, Charlie. But we know there are very few people who really live by the Commandments."

"Yeah, it's a pretty sure thing man hasn't got to the level of civilization where God wants us, Meg. We're still fighting each other for power and for things. Don't ya see, even the great religious leaders still fight for power for themselves, not for the people who follow them. They'd rather keep their people in the dark. They care more about themselves and their organizations than their own people.

"And Meg, I think there is a difference between 'Faith' and 'Trust'. To me, faith seems to be more about organized religion, and Trust more about a person's feelings about God."

"Remember, Charlie, from time to time God has sent great prophets like Moses, Samuel, Isaiah, Jesus and Mohammed to remind us that all we have to do is follow His Commandments and trust Him."

"Yeah, I know, I think God is in the heart of man and we will keep on searching for Him.

"On my trips I saw that all people have the same questions I have. Why does God allow evil? Why does He let bad things happen to good people? Why is something evil in one society but okay in another?

Charlie's Tale

"What I think is that God's plans stretch over His unlimited time and space. We little guys with our short time on earth and our small brains can't know His plan. But, He gave us the freedom to choose between good and evil and it's up to us to choose. If we would just keep his Commandments, we'd be headed in the right direction."

"Maybe, Charlie as time passes and man gets more educated and civilized he will not be led so easily by the power hungry or his own evil thoughts. Maybe people will live by The Ten Commandments.

"Now you should be able to understand that the soul is light, Charlie, God's own light, the image in which we were made. The light has always been a part of you, as it is of every living thing, and as your soul has learned and become whole, you again have become a part of God.

"God Is, Charlie, and you have become part of the whole again. That is how you meet God."

"Did we get it through your 'hard head' Charlie", Meg laughed.

"Yeah, I understand, Meg. Instead of blindly following human leaders, we should look up to and follow God."

"You can come with me now, Charlie. Let us become one with God.

The End

Charlie's Tale

AFTERWORD

And so, it is so simple; we have been given ten simple rules. Can the human race learn to live by them? Can you and I learn to live by them?

Charlie's Tale

ABOUT THE AUTHOR

Ann Anovitz lives in Tucson, Arizona. She is a long-time Commercial Real Estate executive, avid community volunteer and a skillful writer.

Ann is currently Chairman at Ann Anovitz Associates. She has successfully practiced commercial real estate for the past thirty-five years, negotiating office and retail leases and selling commercial properties in the Chicago area. Prior to establishing Ann Anovitz Associates in 1982, she worked as sales and the leasing manager for another commercial real estate company and as administrative manager for several architectural engineering and construction firms. Ann holds an BA in Sociology and is a licensed Real Estate Broker.

In addition to *Charlie's Tale*, Ann is the author of the *Grandma Annie's Stories From the Garden*. Children's Book Series. The innovative series is designed to be a unique educational reading experience for both English and Spanish speaking children. With a simple 180 degree flip, the child can move from one version of the story to the other.

The first title of the series, *Cowboy Jose and Pinteroo* was published in August 2014. The second book titled, *Wigga Poo's Soccer Team*, is scheduled to be released in January 2015.

Charlie's Tale

╬RICHER Press
An Imprint of Richer Life, LLC

RICHER Press is a full service, specialty Trade publisher whose sole goal is to *shape thoughts and change lives for the better*. All of the books, eBooks and digital media we publish, distribute and market embrace our commitment to help maximize opportunities for personal growth and professional achievement.

To learn more visit
www.richerlifellc.com.

www.ingramcontent.com/pod-product-compliance
Lightning Source LLC
LaVergne TN
LVHW041615070426
835507LV00008B/248